True Stories (and other lies) Told at City Café

By

Henry Matthew Ward

Copyright ©2016 by Henry Matthew Ward
Library of Congress Control Number: 2016914161

ISBN 978-0-9814913-4-9

Murfreesboro, Tennessee

Printed in the United States of America

Dedicated to the owners of City Café, both Past, Present, and Future. You hold the heart of Murfreesboro, the pulse of a city. Thank you for giving us nourishment . . . not only of the body, but of a community soul.

Contents

Foreword	7
Jim Stankwytch	10
Larry Tolbert	11
Marion Bean	13
Jim Rungee	16
Joe Harrison	18
Allen Richardson	20
Nelson Smotherman	23
Dwight Hancock	26
Dr. Bob Womack	28
Andy Womack, Bob Parks	30
Avent Lane	32
Fred Goodwin	35
Bill Carey	37
Bill Nelms	39
Blake Tidwell	42
Don Wiseman, Mayor Hollis Westbrooks	43
Bob Suddarth	44
Bob Lamb, Lee Pate	45
C. Ray Carter	47
Charlie Pitts	50
Norris Lovvorn	52
David Loughry, Lee Victory	55
Curtis (Bubba) Hutson	57

Dan Whittle 59
Pettus Read 60
Dawson Wimsat 61
Delmer & Justin Lowe 64
Everette Smothers 69
Fayne Haynes 71
Terry Noah 74
Hank Ward 75
Chuck Clark 77
Harvell Price 79
Jack Lisi 81
Jack Miller 82
Joe Wolfe .85
Jerry Gaither 86
Jerry Benefield 87
Joel Jobe .88
Bill Cunningham 90
Scott (D.C.) Daniel Sr, D.C. (Jim) Daniel Jr,
Scott Daniel 92
Larry Sims 96
Matthew Royal 100
Mort Cohen 100
Herschel Mullins, Charles Mullins (the jeweler) . 102
Randall Chaudoin, Charles Mullins (the preacher),
Jim Avaritt 108
J.D. Kennedy 113

Robert Holt	115
Truman Jones	117
Ron Williams	119
Dan Austin, Harold Nipper, Dave Robertson	121
Tom Brown	123
Tom Haynes, Johnny Jones	125
John Parker	127
Karon Robinson, Sharon Matheny	131
B.B. Gracy	134
Henry Lane	136
Randy Smotherman	136
John Farmer	138
Drs. David & Lorraine Singer	140
Marvin Briley	141
Bill Shacklett, Richard (Dick) Shacklett	143
J. T. Burnett	144
AN OLD MENU	147
Café la Roadkill	150
Politics & Photos	152
10 O'clock Coffee Club	158
Matt Ward	160
A 25th Anniversary	160
Helen Dam's Wrong Turn	162
Insane Asylum	164
Aunt Noval Waits for My Return	167
The Acupuncturist	169

    Sit By Me 171
    Statistics 172
    My Favorite Room 176
    A Scary Florida Golf Course 178
    An Albatross at the VA Golf Course . . . 179
    The Helpful Waitress 182
    Old Age Ain't for Sissies 182
Dwight & Barbara Faircloth 183
One Liners 185
A Brief History of City Café 190
Stifania Tamburo Hayden 199
Ernest & Ethel Watson 200
Brown Sanford, the Roll Man 202
Nadine Cantrell 203
Gary & Pat Simpson 205
Tammy Greer 207

Foreword
(So you can't say I didn't warn you!)

    National Public Radio has a quiz show in which they tell the audience at the outset that *the questions have been painstakingly researched (however, the answers have not)*. In the case of this book, nothing has been painstakingly researched. Some of the stories told here are possibly lies, some of the lies are possibly true.

    I have been a fairly regular customer at City Café for, altogether, almost half a century. I ate supper with college friends there frequently in the early '60s. I returned to Murfreesboro in 1974 and have haunted it ever since.

    City Café has, as long as I have known it, had a thing variously called the *community table*, the *koffee klatch*, the *liars table*, or worse. There are shifts of occupants at the table depending on the time of day.

    There is a picture hanging in the restaurant entitled the 10 O'clock Coffee Club from one era. This is a group of businessmen and retirees that congregated there at mid-morning for a break, to network, or just to enjoy their camaraderie.

    Out of groups such as this have come tales, jokes, and even touchingly true stories that have entertained, informed, brought on guffaws, and sometimes even elicited a serious nod and a surreptitious wiping away of a tear or two.

I have both a blessing and a curse . . . I remember these stories and jokes. What I can't always remember is who told what. So, Reader, the stories you are about to read, though their veracity can't always be affirmed, they will be pretty close to what was said, however they may be mis-attributed, and what was said may be far from the truth. My apologies if I got anything wrong.

I also apologize if I have too many of my own stories included. After all, I was always present for all of them and told them many times, so I remember those best.

I certainly wasn't there all day every day, so I no doubt have missed many good ones. This book will have a second expanded edition if you've got a story to share and will get it to me.

Most of these stories are preceded with a short introduction of the teller. Keep in mind, sometimes what you read within that intro is the real story.

The table of contents refers to whatever name or names are significant in that particular story. Sometimes it is the storyteller's name, sometimes the person the story is about, sometimes both.

Finally, in writing down many of these stories, I was reminded of a poem by Mary Rita Schilke Korzan entitled *When You Thought I Wasn't Watching*. In it she describes things she saw her mother do as she grew up. It ends with . . .

When you thought I wasn't looking, I saw tears come from your eyes, and I learned that sometimes things hurt, but it's all right to cry.

When you thought I wasn't looking, I saw that you cared and I wanted to be everything that I could be.

When you thought I wasn't looking, I looked...and wanted to say thanks for all the things I saw when you thought I wasn't looking.

My sentiments are similar. To those of you who told these tales . . . when you thought I wasn't listening, I listened . . . and I thank you for enriching my life.

+++

Jim Stankwytch

Jim Stankwytch was the only man I ever knew that had a 10-letter last name with only one vowel. (OK, maybe the y is in its "sometimes" role.) Jim was an attorney who worked for State Farm's Regional Office and ultimately became in charge of the claims division. When he retired, he enjoyed coming to City Café and bantering with the morning coffee drinkers.

It was clear from many comments he made over the years that he adored his wife, Janet. One story he told was about her work during WWII at Oak Ridge, Tennessee. Oak Ridge was a top secret town near Knoxville that suddenly was established in 1942 as a production site for the Manhattan Project—the massive American, British, and Canadian operation that developed the atomic bomb. Mrs. Stankwytch was one of the many women employed there who were later characterized in a book as *The Girls of Atomic City* by Denise Kiernan.

Most of the employees working there were only privy to a tiny bit of what was going on. They were on a "need to know" basis. Very few knew they were working on a weapon. However, Mrs. Stankwytch was secretary to one of the most important heads at the site. A lot of top secret information passed through her hands. She was, of course, sworn to secrecy.

Jim said that she wouldn't even tell him anything about her work other than she was a secretary. She did, however, tell him one day a prediction. She said, "Something big is going to happen tomorrow."

Tomorrow came, and Enola Gay flew over Hiroshima, Japan. Something big happened!

+++

Larry Tolbert

Larry Tolbert is a local attorney, MTSU sports announcer, and a fellow who thinks riding 100 miles at a time on a skinny little hemorrhoid-inducing bicycle seat is fun! I remember well his telling of this story at City Café's community table. It was about a rape trial held in Woodbury. To lend an additional degree of authenticity to it, he says he heard it from Judge Wiley Holloway who was the presiding judge at the trial.

The victim was in the witness box and being questioned by the prosecutor.

"Did the accused say anything to you before he accosted you?"

Victim: "He certainly did!"

"What did he say?" he iterated.

"He bragged about what he was going to do to me," the victim replied, sheepishly.

"What were his exact words?" the prosecutor pressed.

"Well, I'm too much of a lady to repeat what he said," she shrugged.

"I completely understand," the D.A. declared. "Perhaps, you could just write it down for our jurors to see," he added as he handed her pad and pen.

She dutifully wrote out what the rapist had bragged he was about to do to her during the attack. The sheet was torn off, properly entered as evidence and passed to the first juror who read and passed it on to the next, and next.

And so it went until it got to a lady juror who, after reading it, found the man next to her had nodded off. He was sound asleep. She nudged him and handed him the note. He read it, looked slyly over to her, smiled and winked, folded the note and put it into his pocket.

+++

Marion Bean

Marion Bean for many years owned a sewing machine shop located on the square. He sold out a few years ago and now lives the life of Riley, if Riley ever lived half a year in Texas and half in Tennessee when he wasn't traveling around in his RV.

I call him Mr. Bean, remembering the British comic, Rowan Atkinson, who created the hilarious *Mr. Bean* TV series.

We have to take everything Mr. Bean says with a grain of salt. After all, the man claims to be in his late 80s but just looking at his slim physique and peppy step, you know he's got to be lying. Can't be over 55!

When Bean was just a sprout and ready to become a businessman, he got a salesman job with a Singer Sewing Machine shop that was located on the south side of the square. (Coincidentally, the very same site that City Café had occupied until 1952.)

He worked there 4 years before deciding he wanted to be an entrepreneur and his own boss. After telling the owner of the Singer Sewing Machine shop that he was quitting, the owner asked what he was going to do. He said he didn't know (but he did).

He soon opened his own sewing machine shop on the east side of the square. He was a go-getter and a clever businessman. I use the term *clever* in the most respectful way . . . not clever *sly*, but clever insightful, forward-thinking, sharp.

He soon made a big sale to the Wilson County Board of Education supplying them with 35 sewing machines for their home economics students. They were fine machines because the schools were still using those 37 years later when he sold his business.

He did routine maintenance on them each year for free. And guess where the young ladies that had learned how to sew on those machines brought their daddies (or later, husbands) when they had finagled a promise to buy them a sewing machine. They wanted one like the one they had learned on! Mr. Bean was only too glad to oblige them.

When he got the 35 machines ordered for the schools, he delivered them and set them up. But, he kept the boxes they had come in and brought them back to the store.

Each day, he would set a bunch of empty boxes out front for the trash pick-up on the square (which is done at night to avoid disruption of traffic during the day).

However, each night, before the trash pick-up had come by, he would go back to the store and bring the boxes back inside.

He kept doing this for weeks. His competitor, and former boss at the Singer store would see the empty boxes Marion was putting out and think his former employee was selling like crazy. The man must have been terribly depressed to think he was being outsold so decisively. He quit the business shortly thereafter. Mr. Bean had sewed up the sewing machine business in this region!

With Marion's half-life in Texas (sounds like he's radioactive, doesn't it?) he told a story of one tourist traveling with a tour bus through the Lone Star State.

The bus stopped at a trading post and the tour group got off. Sitting on the porch of the trading post was an old Indian with a sign above him that said, "This old Indian remembers everything!"

One of the tourists couldn't resist testing the old man's memory and asked him, "If you remember everything, tell me . . . what did you have for breakfast on the morning of January 23rd, 1948?"

The old Indian thought for a moment and then answered, "Eggs."

The tourist realized that wasn't a very good question to test him and was trying to think of a better one that he could somehow verify. But, the tour bus driver called the group back to the bus to resume the trip and he didn't get a chance to quiz the Indian further.

As Mr. Bean tells it, years later, the same tourist was traveling through the same area of Texas, this time on his own. He was walking down a street of a small town when he approached an old Indian sitting outside a barbershop. It was the same old man he had seen years earlier at the trading post. Not recognizing him, he simply held up a palm and repeated the clichéd Indian greeting, "How!"

The old Indian looked up at him and responded, "Scrambled."

+++

Jim Rungee

There is a doctor in town by this name, a literal *sawbones* . . . an orthopedic surgeon. But this next story comes from his father, Lt. Col. (ret.) James L. Rungee, Sr.

After a military career, Jim couldn't just sit around home so he became a Realtor. I had the pleasure of working with Jim for many years at Bob Parks Realty. Jim was the *senior statesman* among us in the office.

Actually, Jim was much more than just a Realtor. Among his many talents, he combined the seemingly incompatible mixture of boxing and piano playing. Even into his 70s, Jim kept a boxing bag hanging in his carport and worked out with it regularly. Yet, he might be found playing requests on the piano at a local road house if the opportunity arose.

Because of his many years stationed in South America with the military, he became fluent in Spanish. This capability made him very useful in later life as Rutherford County acquired more and more Hispanics who did not speak English. He could and did interpret for local police and other officials. In fact, the talent might have been one reason Jim was selected as Grand Jury Foreman for a period of years. No other Spanish interpreter was needed when Jim sat on the Grand Jury.

Now, I'm getting around to Jim's story which has to do with that very capacity . . . translator.

A certain town had a bank robbery. The police caught up with the robber, but not before he had stashed the cash somewhere. The detectives had the suspect in their interrogation room and had to call in an interpreter because the man spoke only Spanish.

One of the officers told the translator to ask him where he hid the money. The go-between asked him in Spanish for the requested information. The suspect answered that he wasn't going to tell them anything.

After relaying that answer to the police, the other detective played his role in "good cop, bad cop ploy" and pulled out his gun, stuck it to the side of the suspect's head and told the translator, "You tell him if he doesn't tell where that money is right now, I'm going to blow his brains out!"

After the translation, the robber spit out (in Spanish) that the loot was in a trash can in the alley behind the bank.

The translator turned to the police and, after a thoughtful pause, said, "He says, you ain't got the guts to shoot!"

+++

Joe Harrison

Joe Harrison and his wife Madelon owned the Big B Cleaners on the square. Lots of people did not know that Joe was also the developer and owner of several motels in the mid-south. Their beautiful vintage home perched on a hill overlooking acreage on Salem Rd. was purchased by World Outreach Church after Joe's passing.

Even though he was a multi-millionaire, he still worked in virtually any role needed at the dry cleaner business on the square. One day, he somehow caught one of his hands in a steam presser that locks down for a set number of seconds on clothing that is being pressed. The injury to his hand was extreme. The pain must have been unbearable. His hand never regained its normal appearance or usability.

Nevertheless, he continued to come into City Café with a smile and greeting, and sometimes . . . a good story to tell.

Joe told the story of an American lady who was visiting Paris. She was convinced the French hated Americans. They were consistently rude and curt to her. She had grown to expect it when she entered one shop and started perusing the clothes on the racks. A man came over to her and asked in a very impatient tone if he could help her. She declined and continued to browse on her own.

Pretty soon she noticed all the clerks in the store were staring at her. Did they think she was going to shoplift or what? Finally, she had had enough of their haughty attitude and turned abruptly and left the store.

As she was going out the door, she looked back and noticed a sign above the doorway . . . *Nettoyeurs à sec* . . . Dry Cleaners.

+++

Allen Richardson

Allen Richardson used to come in City Café regularly, but since selling his optical dispensary that was affiliated with Dr. Joseph Bailey's ophthalmology practice, he must be spending all his time on the golf course. He's not just a player, though.

Because he has schooled himself so well in the rules of the sport of golf, he has been a dedicated volunteer and professional judge for golf tournaments all over the country, but especially here in his home state. During the 100th anniversary of the Tennessee Golf Association he was named as one of the 50 most influential individuals in this state's golfing history. He was also inducted, last fall, into the TSSAA (Tennessee Secondary Schools Athletic Association) Hall of Fame.

When a golf tournament competitor asks for an interpretation of a rule that might affect what that golfer does next, Allen is the man who will tell him what his options are. He remembers the sometimes

critical little words in the golf rules like *may, must, should, a, the* ! He knows the rules book of golf so well, he can quote chapter and verse for virtually any infraction no matter how obscure. For example, even if you consider yourself an experienced golfer, would you know the rules regarding these situations?
1. Can you spit on your clubface before playing a shot? (Yes, to clean it, but no if you're trying to reduce spin to hit a straighter shot.)
2. If your club head falls off during the swing, and you complete the swing but miss the ball, does it count as a stroke? (If it drops off on the way up in the backswing, no; but if it drops off during the downswing, yes.)
3. If your shot ends up in the clubhouse and the clubhouse is not considered out of bounds, what are your options? (You can open a window or door and try to play through without penalty, or you can pick it up, walk out and take a drop in the appropriate area with a penalty stroke.)

Quoting from a tribute to Richardson in the book *Titans of the TGA* (Tennessee Golf Association), TSSAA director Ronnie Carter said:

I remember one time a coach [from the TSSAA] stood up and asked Allen why the kids had to play the ball down [meaning play it as it lies regardless of whether there is no grass under it, it lies in a divot, or on a tree root for example]. He said, "Coach, you get seventy-two strokes in the game of golf. Eighteen of them we're gonna let you put the ball on a tee. Thirty-six of them are on the green, and we're gonna let you pick it up and clean it. All we're asking you to do is leave it alone for eighteen shots."

Allen told a bunch of golf jokes involving smart-aleck caddies, such as:
Player: "Where'd it go?"
Caddie: "Left."
Player: "How far left?"
Caddie: "When you see Nancy Pelosi, you're getting close."

Player: "What should I hit?"
Caddie: "Try the fairway."

Player: "Can I get there with a 5-iron?"

Caddie: "Eventually."

Golfer hits another hooked drive.
Caddie: "You know the greens fee does include fairways."

Golfer: "I'm playing so badly I feel like jumping into that pond and drowning myself!"
Caddie: "Do think you could hold your head down long enough?"

Golfer (after enduring several caddie zings): "You must be the worst caddie in the world!"
Caddie: "No, sir! That would be too big a coincidence!"

+++

Nelson Smotherman

About 20 years ago, one of my former high school teachers saw me and said, "Matt, you look just like you did in high school!" I replied, "You mean I looked like a fat 50-year old in high school?"

But Nelson does look like he did in high school! At least in trim physique and dark hair. It belies his 83 years.

Nelson worked for the post office until his retirement. Ironically, and sadly, all the healthy walking he did in those years has been replaced with tortuous steps that make him appear he is stepping high trying to keep a 6" snowfall out of his shoes. The cause is neuropathy.

Now, back to Nelson's story. In addition to being a postman, Nelson has for years been a statistician. Specifically, he kept up with the many statistics involved in sport games such as basketball, baseball, football. He was a silent partner in radio broadcasting of sports games. Working for several different radio stations at various times, he would sit with the sportscaster and feed him such information as how many yards the fullback that just ran the last play has racked up for the season. Or who holds the record for most three-pointers in a single basketball game. He's a walking encyclopedia of statistics.

He's also a walking historian when it comes to remembering the Murfreesboro downtown of his youth. Nelson tells a story about being a friend of Maurice and Pauline McKnight when they owned the City Café from 1954 to 1967. Maurice was also the assistant postmaster and, remember, Nelson worked at the post office.

Nelson used to come in the back door of City Café walk through the kitchen and get a plate of food, then proceed to the front where he would sit with friends.

One day, the health inspector dropped in unexpectedly and found Nelson in the kitchen. Back in those days, all kitchen help and wait persons had to have an up-to-date health card showing they had been checked by a physician and deemed to be without disease.

The health inspector asked to see Nelson's card. Owner Maurice McKnight was there at the time and about had a heart attack for fear he might get a bad rating or even shut down for the infraction of having an undocumented person around the food prep area.

However, Nelson calmly opened his wallet and pulled out a valid health card! He had been working part time at a competitor's restaurant (Vincent DeGeorge's), but still came to City to eat with friends.

Around Christmas one year, Nelson came in and ordered a glass of boiled custard that City Café was offering during the season. He remarked, after the waitress poured it, that he wished she had some "flavoring" for it. The waitress, Mrs. Weatherly (wife of Aubrey Weatherly who was the blind man that ran the concession stand at the courthouse for years), went over to the cupboard and came back with a bottle of Jack Daniel's hidden in her apron from which she poured him a shot. Boy, those waitresses sure know how to fatten a tip.

+++

Dwight Hancock

Dwight Hancock dressed impeccably when he was an executive with of First Tennessee Bank. He attributed that to his wife who picked out all his clothes for him. She has the good ole southern name of Mary Forrest which is how Dwight always refers to her. It's not southern because it's *Forrest*, and certainly not because it's *Mary*. It's southern because it's a double name, like Peggy Sue, Sara Jane, or Laura Belle. I just love double names on southern gals.

Now that Dwight's retired, he's a gentleman farmer dabbling with the old family farm out Lascassas Pike.

Dwight is also an inveterate hunter and fisherman. He doesn't just seek local trophies. He goes to South America to fish for big exotic bass. And he flies to South Dakota for an annual pheasant hunt with a few buddies. Being a sportsman of this nature, his story involved a duck hunter.

    A hunter shot a duck that fell across a fence into a neighboring field. The hunter started climbing the fence to retrieve his game when the farmer showed up that owned the field.

    "Where do you think you're going?" the farmer demanded.

    "I was just climbing over to get that duck I shot." responded the hunter.

    "Oh, no you ain't! That's my duck now!"

    "What do you mean, 'your duck'? I brought that duck down!" protested the hunter.

    "But, it's MY FIELD!" countered the farmer. "However," he continued, "we have a way of settling this kind of dispute around here."

    "How's that?" asked the suspicious hunter.

    "Well, first I kick your butt, then you kick my butt, then I kick yours again . . . and so on until one of us gives. The winner gets the duck."

    The hunter eyed the scrawny, little farmer and figured he could take whatever that munchkin could dish out and then give twice as much in return. This was going to be fun. "Fine!" said the hunter. Kick away!"

The farmer might have once been the punter for the Tennessee Titans because he put a well-aimed boot on the hunter's back side that managed to center right on the man's groin area.

The hunter fell to the ground and writhed in agony for several minutes until he finally recovered and got up. With an evil smile on his face he said, "All right, now it's MY turn!"

"Nope." The farmer replied, "I give. You can have the duck."

+++

Dr. Bob Womack

Dr. Bob Womack taught in the education department at MTSU for well over 50 years. He had attended there as an undergrad student in his youth and consequently had been a classmate of the parents of many of his later students. Because of knowing him personally, several of his old classmates might call him up when their son or daughter was having some academic troubles and seek his advice.

One, in particular, he told about in the City Café Kaffee Klatch involved a boy that had flunked out at the end of his first semester. The boy's father called

Dr. Bob and asked if he could figure out what the problem was. The elder pedagogue asked the man what his grades were. The father explained that the son had received an F in everything except geography in which he had received a D.

"Well, there you have it!" responded Dr. Womack. "The boy was clearly spending too much time on geography!"

Sometimes, male teachers in a university situation receive too much admiration and attention from young, impressionable female students. Sometimes, these students even try to influence the teacher's grades for them by flirting and even trying to seduce the teacher. Dr. Womack told of one sultry co-ed that came in for a consultation with her professor.

"Oh, Doctor Womack," she whispered in her breathy Marilyn Monroe voice, "I'd do anything to get an A in your class."

Bob knew what she meant, but said innocently, "Anything?"

She responded with a smile, "Yes, absolutely anything!"

The professor moved closer, smiled and whispered in her ear, "Would you study?"

+++

Andy Womack
Bob Parks

Andy Womack, of the State Farm agency, is the son of the aforementioned Dr. Bob Womack, and sometimes ate with his father at City and occasionally dropped in at City Café sans pater. Just like his dad, he knows, and can tell, a lot of tales, most of them true. Like the one about his friend (and my favorite boss, having worked nearly 25 years for him) Bob Parks.

Most people that have been around Murfreesboro any length of time know, or know of Bob Parks. Not all know that he wasn't born with a silver spoon in his mouth. His mother was widowed when Bob was just a toddler. To make ends meet, she became a housemother at one of the dormitories on the MTSU (then MTSC) campus. Bob grew up in a little apartment in a dormitory. When he graduated from Central High School, he was back on the MTSU campus as a student.

Years later, after working a short time at State Farm, he was a real estate agent, first with Clark Maples Realty and then as the broker of his own agency.

Once he was called to court to testify regarding a real estate transaction that had ended up in dispute.

While he was on the stand, he was asked what he had observed about the defendant during his dealings with him.

Bob testified that the defendant had seemed nervous and evasive. The defendant's lawyer jumped on this and asked what expertise did Mr. Parks have to evaluate another person's demeanor or disposition.

In typical Bob Parks' humility, he looked down and said, "None, I guess. Oh . . . I do have a degree in psychology." This is another example of Defense Law 101 . . . Be careful of asking questions of which you don't already know the answer.

Why has Bob Parks been so successful? Andy says, besides being a nice guy with a great personality, he's willing to take a chance. Womack says that he, Bob and two other close friends who all worked at State Farm at the time were all down in Florida and were attending their first dog races. In Florida, they bet on which greyhound can chase a mechanical rabbit to the finish line first, just like pari-mutuel horse races. The four of them and their wives were at the $1 window ready to place a bet . . . all except Bob.

Where's Bob, Andy asked Bob's wife.

"Is there a higher stakes window?" she asked in reply.

"Yeah, there's a $20 window." one of them answered.

"I guarantee you, that's where he is!" she said.

This was years ago when the four men were just starting out and making a measly $2 an hour. $20 would have been over a day's wages for any of them. Such was the risk taking fervor of Bob Parks.

Fortunately, he knew more about real estate risks than he did about dogs. People used to think he had the Midas touch. But he hit a few clunkers in an effort to diversify. The Catfish Shack is still a sore memory for him. As long as he sticks with anything real estate related . . . bet on him!

+++

Avent Lane

Avent Lane occasionally quotes that Grand Ole Opry legend, Minnie Pearl, by warning newcomers to the table that he doesn't repeat gossip, "So, listen carefully the first time!"

Avent is a multifaceted person with a wide range of interests and experience. He's been an industrial engineer, an organ and piano technician, string bass musician with various groups such as blue grass, country, folk singers (John Blankenship and the balladeers), and he's been a deputy sheriff.

Truman Jones, our former sheriff for many years tells this story on Avent nearly every time the two of them find themselves at the same table and there's fresh blood to tell it to.

Once, when the two of them were in a patrol car together, Truman (who was in the driver's seat asked Avent to do something that involved Avent's twisting around a bit to see in the back. As he did so, his weight shifted and caused a shotgun that was between them to slide Avent's way. It had been resting with barrel tip on the floorboard and stock up on the bench seat.

When it started sliding toward Avent, it rolled over just enough for the trigger (which was missing a trigger guard) to get caught on the beaded seam of the bench seat. It was the proverbial hair-trigger. The weight of the gun was enough pressure to pull that trigger. The gun went off!

Avent says, he realized immediately what had happened. He thought he had just blown his foot off! His ears were still ringing when he managed to open his eyes enough to peek down at what he was afraid was going to be a stump at the end of his ankle.

He was still whole. And the car had a new hole about the size of a half-dollar in the floorboard. (For those of you who are too young to know or too old to remember what a half-dollar is . . . it's a coin about twice as big as a quarter.)

Even though the car had been sitting still the entire time, there was dust flying around all inside the car. They were in the parking lot of the Sheriff's office. Sheriff Robert Goodwin had just come out when the blast rang out. He walked over to where the sound had seemed to emanate and asked what that noise was.

Avent said he was tempted to say it was backfire from a truck that was passing by, but he just couldn't lie to the sheriff. He said the fear he had just experienced for life and limb, was now replaced with fear of losing his job. But, he added, Truman smoothed things over with the sheriff by taking some of the blame. They both kept their jobs. Truman, as most folks know, eventually got elected sheriff himself upon Sheriff Goodwin's retirement.

Truman's story, of course, is a little different. Truman says he's got a little hearing loss now and that's what did it! He claims the hole in the floorboard was big enough for a man to fall through! He's also pretty sure Avent pulled that trigger to see if the gun was loaded.

Despite the contradictions, the two are still the best of friends. Avent appears (if that's the correct word to use) on Truman's radio show regularly playing his bull-fiddle along with John Blankenship's guitar and mellow voice.

Avent says Truman has the perfect face for radio.

There is even a third version of the shotgun and the hole in the floorboard that is told by Freddie Goodwin. He's the son of former Sheriff Robert Goodwin who was the sheriff when that incident took place. Turns out Sheriff Goodwin was plenty mad at both of them, but I won't belabor that story any further. I do want to tell about Freddie, though. He also comes in City frequently.

+++

Fred Goodwin

Freddie is, among other things, an impresario. He puts together shows. One he brings to town occasionally is the daughter of a couple of movie stars. She talks about growing up with her famous and beloved parents, answers questions from the audience and then screens an old movie or two starring the King of the Cowboys and the Queen of the West. Folks my age know who we're talking about . . . Roy Rogers and Dale Evans!

Freddie is also a record producer. He's done several for RCA and other top labels. Perhaps, his favorite recording group that he worked with was one that is inextricably associated with Roy Rogers . . . The Sons of the Pioneers. Remember, *Cool Waters? Riders in the Sky? Tumbling Tumbleweeds?*

Fred says that, when Roy wasn't fronting the group, the lead singer was Bob Nolan, the handsome one that got most of the dialogue with Roy in the movies.

Fred adds, "When I was a little boy I was always fascinated with Bob Nolan and when I was going to the movie theaters, I was going to see Roy Rogers, but I was thrilled seeing the likes of the Sons of the Pioneers, especially Bob with his unique voice. He looked good and everything. I thought "this guy'll be a star!" This was in the early 50s. I was seeing all the re-releases of the Sons of the Pioneers in the theatres and then they were on television and, actually, that's how they got their recording contract back.

"Roy Rogers, Tim Spencer and Bob Nolan started the Sons of the Pioneers and, if you want to get technical about it, Roy Rogers is the father of cowboy western music as we know it today and he's never been given the credit. Bob sent me his last album and the cover says, *To Fred. The road is a little longer than I'd expected – it is also a little nicer with friends like you along the way – Bob Nolan.*" Boy! You know, when they called me, probably about an hour or so after he died, I cried. I just really loved him."

+++

Bill Carey

This next story is all about longevity. Bill Carey is a Navy veteran who returned to Murfreesboro and became a real estate broker. We go back a long way. When my wife and I returned to Murfreesboro in 1974, we bought the house we still live in from Bill Carey Realty. While I was the percussion instructor in the MTSU music department in the '70s, I taught Bill Jr. drumming.

In 1976, Bill organized a fund raiser golf scramble for the American Diabetes Association, to be played at his new development on South Church Street, *Fox Run* (which later became *Indian Hills*). Now, the scramble also supports the Realtor Scholarship program that assists local high school grads entering college.

At this writing, there have been 39 annual golf scrambles sponsored by Bill, so it's natural that Bill would have told a golf story during one of his many meals at City Café. This one involved another old golfer, Slammin' Sammy Snead and a young man at the time who had just won his first Majors title, Tiger Woods.

The year was 1997. Tiger Woods was 22 years old, while Sammy was 85. Yet, the two of them were playing a round of golf together. They came to a hole that had a grove of tall oak trees between the tee and the green. Sammy was hitting first and played it safe by following a dog leg bend around the grove.

Then he said to Tiger, "Now, when I was your age, I would have just lined up straight for the green and gone right over those trees!"

Well, Tiger took that as sort of a challenge and felt like he'd have to prove he could do whatever Sammy could do. So, he lined up straight for the green and hit as high and far as he could . . . But, it didn't make it. It dropped down right in the middle of that grove.

Then, as they walked off the tee box, Sammy smiled and added, "'Course, when I was your age . . . those trees weren't but about eight feet tall!"

It's all about longevity!

+++

Bill Nelms

Bill Nelms was an attorney who had his office in a bank building right across the street from City Café, so he came in quite often for lunch or even a morning coffee break.

Bill's wife had been in the hospital in Nashville and recently dismissed. She and Bill were sitting at a table in City when a sweet little lady named Rosemary, who drives a taxi cab in Murfreesboro came in. Bill told her he almost called her to go to Nashville to pick up his wife at the hospital because he was busy. Instead, he arranged for her to take the bus to Murfreesboro and she made it OK because it was air-conditioned.

Rosemary told him she would have gladly gone to Nashville to get her. Bill left the table and never indicated he was joking about the matter.

As Rosemary was leaving, she stopped at Bill's table and told his wife to never ride that bus again. Anytime she needed a ride from the hospital – just call her.

Bill was a big story teller and had a particular idiosyncrasy when he told one. At some point, he would pause and look silently out the window for so long that one wondered whether that was the end of the story or if he had forgotten what came next. He had a way of storytelling, though that made the listener want to hear more, so we would patiently wait for him to continue, and we were rarely disappointed.

Bill was a graduate of the University of Tennessee Law School and was a consummate fan of UT sports. One time he told a story that was especially appropriate to be told in a restaurant like City.

It seems a Tennessee recruit and an Alabama recruit were good friends and were traveling together one summer between school sessions. They went into a restaurant, sat down, and the waitress came over to get their order.

The Tennessee boy said, "I'll have some 'maters and some 'taters and some 'lasses."

The waitress immediately exclaimed, "You're from Tennessee aren't you!"

"Yeah," the boy replied, "How could you tell?"

"Why I can just tell from the way you talk." She smiled.

Now, at this point, Bill paused and looked out the window for the longest, while we wondered if there was more to this story. Finally, Bill continued . . .

Well, eventually the boys finished their meal and got back on the road. But, the Alabama boy just kept shaking his head in disbelief saying, "I can't get over how that waitress could tell where you were from just from three little words! I wonder if they could do that with me."

Looking down the road, he said, "Pull in this place over here and let me try that."

They pulled in, went inside, and the Alabama boy blurted out, "I want some 'maters, some 'taters, and some 'lasses."

The man to whom he had given his request responded, "You're from Alabama, aren't you!"

"Yeah," grinned Alabama. "How could you tell?"

Another long pause by Nelms . . .

"'Cause this is a HARDWARE STORE!"

+++

Blake Tidwell

Blake Tidwell, of Bell Jewelers, used to come sit at the community table regularly back when his jewelry store was on the square. Among the many stories he told, one was especially apropos because it dealt with a jewel.

Blake claimed that he complimented a widow lady on the beauty of a large diamond ring she was wearing.

"Yes," she replied. "My late husband gave me this. Well, actually he took out a $10,000 life insurance policy to cover his funeral expenses and memorial stone when the time came. He told me to spend $5,000 for the burial, and $5,000 for the stone." Wiggling her ring finger, she added, "and this here's the stone."

Another story of Blake's involves an older man who came into his jewelry store one time with a good-looking younger woman on his arm. He told Blake that he wanted to buy her something "real nice" and pointed to a case full of diamond bracelets.

"Honey," he said, "you can have anything you want on this shelf here." He pointed to a shelf with several 5-figure diamond bracelets on it. She giggled, and picked the most expensive one of the lot.

The man told Blake he'd write a check for it, but said he understood that the bracelet couldn't be taken out of the store until the check cleared. Blake confirmed that was the policy. The couple left with the agreement the customer would come back in Monday to pick up the bracelet.

Monday came, and the man showed up. Immediately, Blake said, "Sir, that check of yours wasn't any good at all!"

The man replied, "Yeah, I know. I just came back in to thank you for a fantastic weekend!"

+++

Don Wiseman
Mayor Hollis Westbrooks

Don Wiseman was a city councilman for several years, and a regular at City Café. Don told the story of a classic spoonerism that Mayor Westbrooks committed about 1975 in his opening remarks to those in attendance and listening over the radio at the ribbon cutting ceremony for Old Fort Parkway, the four-lane divided road that was to become the gateway into Murfreesboro from Interstate 24 for the next 35 years. The laughter lasted longer than the speech when the straight-laced Mayor started out with, "Well, we are just so proud to be out here for this grand opening on *Old Fart Porkway* . . ."

+++

Bob Suddarth

Bob Suddarth was clerk of court for many years. During lunch breaks in court, Bob would frequently enjoy his at City Café. I'm telling this next story on myself, but it's about Bob. We were both seated at the community table when the subject of the Lion's Club had come up. I used to belong to the Lion's club and told about a funny thing that happened at one of our weekly meetings.

We always started out the formal part of the meeting by standing and reciting the Pledge of Allegiance. A different member would be called upon to lead the pledge each week.

On one particular occasion, (I explained I couldn't remember who the leader of the day was) but we all stood up, faced the flag, put our right hand over our heart and waited for the leader pro tem to start us off. Then, out of his mouth came the classic faux pas, "Our Father, who art in heaven..."

Everyone at the community table laughed . . . except Bob. He sat in silence with face downcast, just shaking his head. "Yep!" he said, "That was me!"

+++

Bob Lamb
Lee Pate

Lee Pate was a regular at the community table of City Café for many years. He was a legendary men's football and basketball coach at the old Central High School.

Bob Lamb is the owner/broker of Exit Realty in Murfreesboro. Before that, I had the privilege of being his colleague at Bob Parks Realty for many years. Bob and his good friend, Bud Morris, are loyal MTSU alumni and the strongest of Blue Raider Athletic Association members. They attend all the home football games and many of the away games.

Bob told the story of sitting at the City Café community table with Bud one day when the subject of college football came up. That particular year, the University of Miami (Florida) team was a great one. Someone was talking about them and, as Bob puts it, "I had to pop off the little bit of trivia that MTSU was 2-

0 against the Hurricanes. Knowing that I would be the only one at the table (except Bud Morris) that would know this, I was sure I would astound the others with my vast knowledge of football!

"Just when someone was telling me that I didn't know what I was talking about, Mr. Pate looked up from his cup of coffee and says, 'Yes, that's right. I threw the winning touchdown pass in 1932.'

"We were all in awe! Just for the record, the Middle Tennessee State Teachers College took the long train ride down there on consecutive years, 1931 and 1932, with only about 19 members, and came back winners both times!"

Hardly anyone in real estate has a degree . . . in real estate. Bob Lamb has a degree or two from MTSU in biology. It was probably this interest that caused Bob to tell the following story about a biologist who did an experiment with a frog.

First, he taught the frog to jump on his command, "Jump!" Once he had the frog well trained, he put the frog on a line and said, "Jump, frog!"

The frog jumped 8 feet, which the scientist duly recorded in his journal. Then . . . he cut off one frog leg! He again put the frog on the line and said, "Jump, frog!"

The frog jumped 6 feet. He wrote in his journal, "Cut off one frog leg and frog loses 25% of jumping ability." Then . . . he cut off another leg, put the frog on the line and said, "Jump, frog!"

The frog jumped 4 feet. He wrote in his journal, "Cut off two frog legs and frog loses 50% of jumping ability." Then . . . he cut off a third leg. Same routine.

The frog jumped 2 feet. He records, "Cut off three frog legs and frog loses 75% of jumping ability. Then . . . he cut off the forth leg, put the frog on the line and said, "Jump, frog!"

The frog just sat there. Once again the biologist commanded, "Jump, frog!" The frog just sat there.

"JUMP, FROG!" he shouted. But the frog just sat there. So the scientist writes in his journal, "Cut off all four frog legs and frog *loses hearing!*"

+++

C. Ray Carter

C. Ray Carter came here from Virginia where he owned an office supply company. He sold his business and came to Murfreesboro because he was involved in Tennessee Walking horses and we are in the heart of that sporting industry. C. Ray (as we all called him) has recently turned 90. Widowed a few years ago, he eventually took up with a nice lady though he wouldn't marry her. She was 28 years younger than he. He told his doctor that he was "re-living his youth" (to put it delicately) with his girl-friend. The doctor told him that sort of living could be fatal. His reply, as he related to the coffee klatch was, "Well, if she has to go, she has to go!"

After a hearty laugh, we nevertheless raised an eyebrow at the implication. That's when C. Ray told the following story:

A 65-year old man was getting a physical from his doctor who, after the exam, told him he was in excellent shape for a man of 65. Then the doctor asked, "How old was your father when he died?"

"Did I say my father was dead?" the man replied indignantly.

"Oh, I beg your pardon," apologized the doctor. "How old is your father?"

"My father is 85 and plays golf every day!"

"Well," the doctor commented, "You obviously have some good genes. So, how old was your grandfather when he died?"

"Did I say my grandfather was dead?" the man again huffed.

"Your *grandfather* is still living?" the doctor said with surprise.

"My grandfather is 104 and getting married again next Friday!" the man said proudly.

"104! And getting married at his age!" Then the doctor asked incredulously, "What does a 104-year-old want to get married for?"

The man grinned and answered, "Did I say, 'he *wanted to?*'"

C. Ray is noted for his generosity. He always leaves a whole quarter tip whether he had a full meal or just a cup of coffee. Has a big, booming voice, too. Combined with a total disdain for political correctness or genteel language, he comes out regularly with some colorful pronouncements that would cause everyone at the table to cringe. He used to spend half a year here in Murfreesboro, and the other half in Florida. Recently, however, he sold his house here and moved to Florida year-round. I'm surprised, though. According to C. Ray, "There's too many Damn Yankees in Florida!"

C. Ray said he dressed up as a KKK member for Halloween one year. Bill Sellers said C. Ray was so short he only needed a pillowcase for his costume.

C. Ray asked Fran, the waitress, if she'd like to go to Louisiana with him in his motor home. She said she didn't ride with anyone that had to stand up to drive.

Someone asked C. Ray, "At what age does the sex drive go away?"

He said, "I don't know. You'll have to ask someone older than me."

Then they asked, "How is it you're so healthy for a man of 90?"

He explained, "It's because I never drank, or smoked, or fooled around with women until I was 10 years old."

+++

Charlie Pitts

Charlie Pitts is a *coiffeur*, which is a fancy word for *hair dresser*, which is a fancy term for *barber*. Charlie says the difference is about $50,000 a year. And, *barber* does seem just too plain a word for Charlie. He is so gregarious, when he comes to City, he'll sit near the front and greet each customer that comes in after him to the extent they think *he's* the proprietor!

He loves to tell stories, and often tells them on himself. After a while, people who get to know him listen with deserved skepticism. A story that originally started, "This man goes into a bar . . ." with Charlie becomes, "I went into this bar . . ."

But, we don't mind his personalization of the joke. It makes it all the funnier. Sometimes, however, Charlie's stories are so embarrassing they get the response from one of his punch lines, "Brother, don't think I'd a told that one!"

One time he said he hoped he died peacefully in his sleep like his Uncle John, not screaming and kicking like the other three people in Uncle John's car.

Charlie always carries around a dozen or so keys on a fob. One would think he was an apartment super, or janitor. They are so bulky, he can't carry them in his pocket, so he usually just carries them in his hand when he goes into the restaurant and sets them down on the table in front of him.

One day, when he got ready to leave, the keys were missing from the table. He was convinced someone at the table had pilfered them and hidden them somewhere. He pleaded, cajoled, and demanded, but no one would own up to the deed. Finally, he gave us the benefit of the doubt and went to look in his car to see if he had absentmindedly left them in it.

They weren't there, which convinced him even stronger that one of those so-and-sos at his table had hidden them. He stormed back in and half the restaurant heard him giving our table "what for" while he demanded the return of his keys.

Then . . . he noticed a lump inside his appointment book which had been in his hand all this time. He opened it and out slid the keys.

"Never mind"

+++

Norris Lovvorn

Norris Lovvorn was a bondsman . . . he bonded people out of jail. He was also a baseball fanatic. He kept up with all the pro teams and even some of the little leaguers. He was also a chain smoker. A portrait hangs in City Café to this day that was painted by artist Lisa Sims that captures the essence of Norris with a cigarette in hand (which he was rarely seen without) and smoke rising in a plume above it.

Norris was a Yellow dog democrat and proud of it. The term was applied to voters in the South during the late 19th century who voted a straight Democratic Party ticket. These voters would allegedly "vote for a yellow dog before they would vote for any Republican." Norris once said . . . no, make that *frequently* said, "The worst Democrat is better than the best Republican!"

Garry Simpson, the City Café owner at that time, was a close friend despite being a Republican. They went to baseball games together and kidded around a lot at the restaurant. Garry tells of Norris' knack of predicting what every ball player was going to do on the next play as they watched a game. Once, while at an Atlanta Braves game, the bases were loaded. A batter came up who was not known to be a strong hitter, but Norris said, "Watch. He'll hit a grand slam." And he did. Norris said he saw him do the very same thing when he played for the Nashville Sounds.

Once, Governor Ned McWherter, a democrat, was coming to Murfreesboro on a campaign. He stopped in City Café as politicians frequently do. Judge David Loughry, also a democrat, introduced him to Garry Simpson, the owner.

Governor McWherter was scheduled to speak later that day at another venue in town, and the two prevailed on the governor to make a reference to "his good friend, Garry Simpson."

Later, Garry told Norris about the speech Norris' democrat governor was going to make around the corner and that they should go and hear him.

Of course, Yellow Dog had to be there! He had been a contributor to the governor's campaign. The two of them went and stood together. The usual hyperbole was spoken and various names dropped, but it really galled Norris when McWherter saw the two of them and then recognized and gave praise to "my good friend, Garry Simpson." The republican! No mention of Yellow Dog! Just that Republican!

One time, staunch Republican, Phil Harper, asked Norris Lovvorn, his neighbor, for a ride home from City. Lovvorn said he would if Phil would lie down in the back seat so nobody would see him.

Someone accused Norris of being a closet Republican. He shot back, "If I were a Republican, I would want to be in a closet!"

Sometimes, Norris would sit at the table so long, the waitresses would have cleared away his dishes and he would forget whether he had eaten breakfast or not. Once, he asked the fellows at the table whether he had eaten and, though he had not even given the waitress an order, they convinced him he had eaten his regular meal and it had been cleared away. He left the restaurant thinking he had had his morning meal.

+++

David Loughry, Lee Victory

David Loughry is another of the many attorneys that have frequented City Café. David is also a former General Sessions Judge and walking horse enthusiast. One quirk that David has is liking lots of lemon in his tea. I mean LOTS! It is not unusual for David to squeeze the juice from two, maybe three whole lemons into one glass of iced tea. The waitress knows to bring him a bowl full of sliced lemons when they serve him.

David is another hometown boy and knows everybody. I won't say he's the Bubba of Murfreesboro, but he knows Bubba! He could tell some stories on Bubba, too, but that might incriminate himself.

He did joke that when his friend Bubba Hutson sold his farm and bought a house on Main St. that he was going to write a book titled *Bubba Moves to Main Street*. Seems he saw some promising humor in that. You've got to know Bubba, too, to appreciate the potential.

One story David told recently was about Smyrna legend, Lee Victory. (There's a parkway in Smyrna named after him.)

David saw Lee walking around the public square here in Murfreesboro and greeted him. Lee said he was looking for his car and couldn't remember where he parked it. About 10 minutes later, David saw Lee coming around for the second time. This time Lee said, "Couldn't find my car. Now I'm looking for my truck. Maybe that's what I drove today."

David told a story about another judge. This judge grew tired of seeing the same town drunk in front of his bench. One day the judge glared down at the man, who was still intoxicated, and thundered "It is the sentence of this court that you be taken from here to a place of execution and there hanged by the neck until DEAD."

The drunk promptly fainted. The court bailiff commenced to revive the man, and looked up at the judge, at which time the judge shrugged and responded "I've always wanted to do that."

+++

Curtis Hutson
aka Bubba

Yeah, this is the real Bubba previously mentioned. Bubba is a businessman with the ironic combination of being the owner of a liquor store and a drunk driver school.

Bubba Hutson was raised on a farm just outside of Murfreesboro. When he sold a good chunk of his land for an interstate on-off ramp and more to others wanting to locate businesses adjacent to it, he bought a vintage house on the corner of East Main and Hancock and had extensive work done to it both inside and out. One of the outside improvements, though minor compared to most of his remodeling, was planting boxwoods at the end of his walkway where it intersected with the sidewalk of East Main.

Then he learned that one of the crosses to bear is that many people walk their dog on these Main Street sidewalks. The walkers have a dual purpose. They're out to exercise their dogs and themselves. But most of them are also trying to give their dog the option of using someone else's yard for a restroom instead of their own. The conscientious ones will bring little plastic bags with them and pick up the ugly droppings of their beasts, take them home and dispose of them.

But, believe it or not, some people are not conscientious. In many cases, these same people wouldn't think of throwing trash out their car windows as they drive down Main Street (or any other street), though Murfreesboro is not free of that kind of litter either.

The only defense for the homeowners who (surprise) don't care for the care packages left on their lawns is to either put out a tacky sign, or catch them in the act and tell the dog owner that this isn't appreciated (as if the leash holder was completely oblivious to this possibility).

The other problem Bubba found with dogs on leashes walking by his house involved the boxwoods. They like to hike their leg on one bush or the other... or both!

Now, being a country boy, Bubba had a clever solution for this. He had some experience with electric fences. (Do you see where this is going?)

He bought a cattle fence energizer, hooked up some wire and ran it out to the bushes. He put a couple of small, inconspicuous wooden stakes each side of each bush, stretched a screen-like, almost invisible wire grid between them, attached the energized wire to the screens and turned on a low current that wouldn't kill, but, shall we say, wouldn't be pleasant to the originator of any liquid stream that might strike it.

Bubba said it was amazing how fast an old dog can learn a new trick . . . the trick of looking at his bushes and keep on walking.

Don't look for his contraption now. He's since sold that house and moved to another East Main address, the big house on the corner of Main and Highland that has the two lion statues stretched out on either side of his front door.

+++

Dan Whittle

Dan Whittle is an amiable fellow from Missouri who moved to Smyrna several years ago. He says, when he left Missouri and came to Tennessee, the average IQ of both states went up!

Dan is a reporter, columnist, humorist, author of books and a photographer extraordinaire. Though he has written far more than I have, he delights in saying, "Here comes a *real* author!" every time he sees me enter the café.

The café had a sign on the bulletin board asking for donations to buy Dan a one-way ticket to Afghanistan. When Whittle read it, he commented, "I thank you from the heart of my bottom."

+++

Pettus Read

Pettus Read worked for the Farm Bureau for 44 years. That put him in the midst of a lot of rural stories that he has told in a syndicated newspaper column that has appeared in dozens of newspapers across the state. He published a collection of these stories under the title *Read All About It*. It took me a while to catch the pun in the title. I guess it's one of those college puns that you get by degrees.

He's also a county commissioner, one of the ones that come in to City Café even when they aren't campaigning for re-election.

One day, when we were all reminiscing about our childhoods, the subject of Harvey's escalators and elevators came up. For many of us, Harvey's department store in downtown Nashville was our first introduction to either mode of transportation.

Pettus told the story of a farmer that brought his family in to the big city and saw an elevator for the first time himself. He watched the doors open and a frumpy old lady get on. The doors closed and he waited to see what would happen next. About a minute later, the doors opened again and a beautiful young lady stepped out.

"Son," the old farmer said, "go git yer Ma!"

Pettus commented on the new state law allowing grocery stores to sell wine. He says it means that, in addition to liquor stores, the Baptists won't be able to recognize each other in Kroger's now either!

+++

Dawson Wimsat

Dawson Wimsat owned the upscale tobacco shop next door to City Café for several years, so he might pop in at any time of the day. He was always an interesting addition to the table because he had such a wide range of knowledge. Dawson was our "Google" before the internet. We couldn't get away with much when Wimsat was at the table. Case in point:

I'm more of a writer than a talker. Give me time to think and choose the right word and I can sound a lot more intelligent than I really am, although I wouldn't say I was as taciturn as Calvin Coolidge was noted to be. In fact, (to digress a moment) one story about Coolidge involves a state dinner in which a movie star was assigned a seat next to the president. Early in the meal, the actress turned to the president and teasingly said, "Mr. President, I have a bet with my husband that I can get you to say more than two words tonight."

Silent Cal, as he had been dubbed by the press, turned to her and said, "You lose!"

Anyway, as I was saying, no one has ever accused me of monopolizing the conversation. One day, when I must have been particularly reserved, one of the others seated at the table said, "Matt, you don't say much, do you?"

I replied with the witticism, "I believe, as Mark Twain once said, that it is better to remain silent and be thought a fool, than to open one's mouth and remove all doubt."

Dawson quickly responded, "Matt, it was Abraham Lincoln that said that."

See what I mean? Shoulda kept my mouth shut!

Dawson told deep jokes. Sometimes they were so deep nobody caught it. Like the story about a man that was building a brick barbeque grill on his patio. When he finished, he had one brick left over. So, he shrugged his shoulders and just tossed it over his privacy fence that paralleled a busy street.

Now, we're all waiting for the punch line. Who did it hit? What ironic damage did it cause, or something. But, that's it . . . end of story. Was this just another one that was too deep for any of us to catch? Eventually, he started up another story. This one had some relevance to his cigar store enterprise.

"A man was sitting on a city bus next to a lady who had a little dog in her lap," began Wimsat. "After a few blocks, the man pulled a stogie out of his vest coat, stuck it in his mouth and lit up."

"The lady stared indignantly at him and finally reached over, jerked the cigar out of his mouth and hurled it out the window. The man looked incredulously at her and then the dog. He quickly reached over, grabbed the dog and hurled it out the window!"

"The lady screamed for the bus driver to stop the bus. She rushed down its steps in fear for her little pooch . . . only to see the dog trotting towards her, no worse for the wear. And guess what it had in its mouth?" Wimsat smiled.

"The cigar!" we all shouted in unison, proud we could finally anticipate the punch line to one of his jokes.

"Nope," the master of obfuscation responded. "The brick!"

+++

Delmer & Justin Lowe

Delmer Lowe and his son, Justin, come in for breakfast about four times a week. There are few father-son relationships closer than theirs. Delmer has a degree from MTSU in agriculture and a master's from UT, and has done well in the cattle business. His farm is out in the Christiana area. His wife has three degrees and works at MTSU, but probably doesn't have to work at all.

But, it's their son Justin I want to tell you about. He graduated from The Webb School, a private school in Bell Buckle. He earned his Eagle Scout award at the troop at First Baptist Church where my son, Jeff Ward, was an assistant scoutmaster. Jeff, told me Justin was one of the most polite young men he had ever known.

Justin just finished a degree in Forensic Anthropology at MTSU where he was often mistaken for one of the professors by other students. This might have been partially because of his mature good looks with a bearded Earnest Hemmingway appearance, and because he frequently wore a sport coat and tie to class . . . a remnant habit from his days at Webb?

Justin is a world traveler. He has been to more countries in his 24 years (at this writing) than most people will get to in a lifetime. We get to hear stories of his experiences each time he comes back. A lot of these trips have been in conjunction with special travel-trip classes offered by MTSU. He was fortunate enough to have parents who could afford to let him gain this experience.

I asked him once how many country stamps he had on his passport. He thought a moment and then started listing, in addition to Israel twice, Spain, France, Ireland, Scotland, Costa Rica, Taiwan, Fiji, and Viet Nam.

He says one country that doesn't stamp passports is Israel because they fear they will put the traveler in jeopardy if and when they subsequently have to show it in one of the Arab countries. Israel is also more cautious about letting people into their country. Each arrival goes through a vetting process that involves speaking, sometimes at length, with a customs official. I have personally experienced this just getting back into the U.S. from Canada. It was obvious the American border guard was really just trying to listen to my accent to see if he detected anything that wasn't consistent with what my passport said. A Russian accent on a guy from Tennessee would have raised a red flag. (No pun intended.)

    Anyway, Justin said that traveling into and out of Israel on more than one occasion, he experienced unusual treatment. Not hard suspicious treatment . . . just the opposite. He would be asked a couple of questions for accent identification, but as soon as they asked him his last name and he responded, "Lowe," the interview was over! He was respectfully handed his passport and allowed to continue through. His fellow traveler, however, might have had to endure several more minutes of vetting. Eventually, he found out the reason for his V.I.P. treatment.

    He found out that *Lowe* was the Germanic or Yiddish variant of the most respected of Jewish names, *Levi*. The Levites were the priests of the Old Testament, and even today, in the Promised Land of the Jews, the name *Levi* (*Lowe*) is revered.

    This brings up the story I told once at City regarding, "What's in a name?" Pope John the XXIII was beloved even among the Jews. His simple greeting endeared himself to them when, in 1960, about two years after his elevation to the papacy, he requested a meeting with world Jewish leaders. But to appreciate the deep significance of his first words to them, we must first recall the story of Joseph and his brothers from the Old Testament.

Joseph, you may remember from Sunday School lessons, was his father's favorite. Jacob (Israel) loved him and spoiled him, much to the jealousy of his brothers...all of whom along with Joseph were to eventually become the patriarchs of the twelve tribes of Israel.

When Joseph was 17, his older brothers sold him into slavery and he was taken away to Egypt. They told their father he had been devoured by a wild animal. For the next 22 years, Joseph rose from slave to the Pharaoh's right-hand man through his ability to interpret dreams and subsequently administer the land for the pharaoh.

During a terrible famine in Canaan, his brothers came to Egypt to buy food. They were directed to the royal storehouse where Joseph recognized them, although they didn't realize who he was. After all, he was then 39 years old and speaking fluent Egyptian.

He tested them to see if they still retained the evil ways of their youth. He hid his silver goblet among the bags of Benjamin, the youngest, then arranged for him to be "caught" with the contraband. He had all eleven of them arrested but then told them he would allow all but Benjamin to return to Canaan and take their purchased food and grain with them.

The brothers refused to abandon Benjamin, and Judah asked that he be taken as a slave in his place. That is when Joseph was convinced they had repented from their earlier treacherous ways. He secluded himself in a room with his brothers, and cried out: "I am Joseph . . . your brother!"

Now, move forward 4000 years and comprehend the significance of the words of Pope John XXIII (whose secular name, by the way, was Joseph Roncalli) as he greeted his Jewish counterparts, rabbinical scholars of the Old Testament who knew the story well. When the leaders entered the room, Pope John's first words to them were, "I am Joseph . . . your brother."

+++

Everette Smothers

Sergeant Everette Smothers, or Sarge (as he was affectionately called), was an enigma. That's a person who is both a policeman, carnival owner and licensed mortician. (He was proud of the fact that he had helped bury Sergeant Alvin York, the most decorated soldier of WWI and a Tennessee native.) How many men with Sarge's qualifications do you know?

Officer Smothers had a tough-man persona, sort of a Humphrey Bogart, James Cagney, Clint Eastwood combination, but he had a heart of gold. Well, maybe silver . . . all right, *copper*, but copper is still a valuable commodity!

He dressed to the nines! He was the only policeman I've ever seen, when in uniform, wore a cravat . . . a white silk muffler-like neckwear that was puffed up in front and tucked under his open collar shirt. He was a cool dude.

Smothers gave me a parking ticket one time for parking in a handicap zone. "But, Sarge, it was a bank parking lot and it was Sunday. The bank wasn't open.

"Don't matter!" Ah, the words and logic of an incorruptible public servant! But, Everette Smothers did have a secret heart of gold. I know of one instance I can't and won't tell about because it involves another person whose image I would not wish to tarnish. Everette could have arrested him and perhaps ruined him for life, but he let him off with a warning. Yes, Everette Smothers was an enigma.

Now, to the story he told . . .

I guess the mortician in him brought out this morbid tale of a hearse that was going up a steep hill on one of San Francisco's streets. Suddenly, the rollers underneath the casket inside slipped out of their locked position and the casket rolled backwards and burst through the double rear doors of the hearse.

It hit the street and kept sliding downhill picking up speed. Finally, at the bottom of the hill where the street ended in a T-intersection, the casket slid right through it, crashed through a door into a drug store, slid all the way back to the druggist's counter where it hit with such force that it popped the lid open and threw the corpse up into a sitting position.

The near-sighted pharmacist looked up and said, "Something I can do for you?" The corpse replied, (wait for it . . . wait for it...) "Yeah. Can you give me something to stop this coffin?"

"Har, har, har!" (That's Smothers, laughing at his own joke.)

+++

Fayne Haynes

Murfreesboro has its share of service veterans. I won't employ the over-used term *heroes*, that takes away from the significance of the true heroes — those that risked life and limb doing extraordinary tasks like storming Omaha Beach on D-Day, fighting in the Battle of St. Lo, or the Battle of Brest, or the Battle of the Bulge. The subject of this next story is, however, a true hero. He did all these things and more. Fayne Haynes regaled us many times at City with tales of his experiences in WWII. He was not reticent as many veterans are to tell his war stories and we were privileged to hear them. Many of us heard the same story more than once, but it was worth it. Worth it, in part to sit at the feet (so to speak) of one of America's greatest generation and hear what it was like from one who lived it. And worth it, too, just to pay homage to one of those to whom we owe so much! It was a duty and it was an honor to listen to him. Below is one of his war stories. To refresh my memory on some of the details, I found an article written by Ken Beck that appeared in the Murfreesboro Post, July 3, 2011. Some of the story below quotes from this article and is used by permission.

He was drafted at the age of 20 and entered as a buck private. Haynes was a gunner in the 612th Tank Destroyer Battalion and among the first to land on Omaha Beach. After fighting their way into France, Haynes' outfit pushed rapidly over 600 miles in an open halftrack to the Siegfried Line between Belgium and Germany. Here, they bogged down and were stuck for 73 days in mud even a halftrack couldn't get through. Thankfully, the German army couldn't get through it either.

"We had to wait until it froze over, and then the Battle of the Bulge started."

On the first day of battle, his crew knocked out three tanks but was soon surrounded by an SS Panther tank unit. That was December 14, 1944.

"There were only 123 of us there, and all were either killed or captured."

Haynes spent four months in a Prisoner of War camp, Stalag XIB, southwest of Hamburg, Germany. By that time, the middle of April, 1945, the Nazis realized they were going to lose the war. Haynes and his fellow POWs were taken from the camp and marched east (away from the approaching American army). About eighty miles into the forced march, during a rest period, Haynes and four of his fellow G.I.s planned their escape.

The German soldiers gave them a 10 minute rest every hour and they would lay beside the road. "When they holler for everybody else to get back in the road, we are gonna lay there and let them walk off and leave us," he told his pals.

"The Germans did just that. They never looked back. They left five of us there. We waited until they were nearly out of sight and got up and walked off."

The danger was not over as the small band had to work its way back toward friendly territory by passing German soldiers and then through the British defense lines where they might mistakenly be shot.

Eventually, they joined with the British army for three days in combat conditions until a mail truck carried them off the front lines. They were flown from Holland over the English Channel to Bristol, England, and then taken to the 318th American Field Hospital where Haynes spent 18 days and put back on 25 pounds.

Mr. Haynes is 94 as I write this in 2016. He has only recently stopped coming to the café due to some health problems, but may soon return. We are ready for another story. God Bless Fayne Haynes and God Bless America.

Sadly, just 5 days after writing the above paragraph, the obituary of Fayne Haynes was published in the local paper.

+++

Terry Noah

Lots of men that frequented City Café (or still do), have nicknames. In some cases, we wouldn't even recognize the person as one of our gang if they mentioned him by his real name. One was Bobby Winn who was known as "Hot Air."

Terry Noah, for example, moved here from Memphis after retirement to be near an adult child and grandchildren who lived here. Because he was recently from Memphis, we called him Elvis. The congenial man didn't look a bit like Presley . . . even had blondish hair, but nevertheless, we called him Elvis. And he brought a fresh bunch of stories with him. (Always helps, to get fresh blood and avoid too much inbreeding of tales.)

From this Elvis we heard tales of the other one. For example:

Elvis Presley was born a twin, the other was stillborn.

On his 11th birthday, Elvis received a guitar . . . it was a terrible disappointment. He was hoping for a bicycle.

The family was very poor. His father was sent to prison for a year for forging a $4 check.

Elvis bought Graceland for $102,500 and it came with 14 acres. Elvis didn't name it Graceland for his mother whom he adored (her name was Gladys, not Grace). It was named by the original owner, Dr. Thomas Moore who had it built in 1939 and named it after his daughter, Grace.

Elvis' controversial manager, Colonel Tom Parker, who claimed to be from West Virginia, was actually a Dutch immigrant who came to America around 1930. He worked as a carnival barker, dog catcher and pet cemetery founder. He talked the governor of Louisiana into being given the honorary title of colonel and insisted thereafter on being referred to as Colonel.

+++

Hank Ward

Another regular with a nickname was the real estate mogul, and a real Colonel, Hank Ward. His real name was Henry G. Ward. He and I were no kin that we know of, but people were always getting our names mixed up. We were both in real estate and both were regulars at City Café. The tendency to mix the names up was compounded by the fact that my first name is also Henry, and its traditional nickname is Hank, but I've always gone by my middle name. Plenty of times, I would walk in and be greeted with "How's it going, Hank?" It never bothered me, but I understand Hank was irritated no end when someone called him, Matt. That's understandable, he was far more successful and good looking so he was being insulted, I wasn't.

    Hank had been an officer in the Army and was still a Lt. Colonel in the National Guard. He had been a helicopter pilot, too. His physique exuded strength with block-buster forearms, plus he had a military bearing about him. He could be very intimidating. He was used frequently to teach rookie real estate licensee's the rules of the Board of Realtors. He was like the cross between a parrot and a tiger. When he spoke, you damn well better listen!

    One of the stories he told was to emphasize that you damn well better get it right, too. He told of a Realtor that showed his customer a vacant house in an area of Nashville that had gone down and consequently had several foreclosures on the block.

The house was a definite fixer-upper, but the price was right and the customer bought it.

The buyer spent thousands of dollars and buckets of sweat fixing it up for re-sale. When he finally had it ready to flip, he called another Realtor to list it. This Realtor did his job and, in the process of looking up tax records, discovered a confusing discrepancy.

It turned out, this man who thought he had bought and fixed up the house at 1424 Dumpy Street, had actually bought another foreclosure at 1426 Dumpy Street. (Few of the houses in that depressed area displayed house numbers. His first Realtor had taken him to the wrong house! He bought 1426 thinking he had bought 1424. He did all his work on the wrong house! The bank that owned 1424 was very happy to find the elves had cleaned up and fixed up their inventory. The final outcome was not disclosed in this Hank Ward story, but the point was made. Don't screw it up; do your homework; pay attention to detail!

+++

Chuck Clark

Chuck Clark has a stentorian voice that has such depth and resonance that it just commands attention.

He's married to a physician who decided to keep her own last name as many professionals do after marriage. After all, she had already established a reputation under her maiden name . . . Dr. Suma Kathleen Clark. That's right! She was already a Clark. Named after her mother, who was director of the MTSU Publication and Graphics department for over 30 years. Her father, Roy Clark, was also a doctor, but "not the kind that can help you," as a little boy once described his professor dad. Roy was a physics professor. Pretty good genes here!

    I've told Chuck he ought to be a host on one of those radio talk shows. He's got the sound of an announcer and the intelligence to talk knowledgeably with any caller on most any subject. He's articulate, too. Unlike me, he can spit out several sentences of confident facts without the slightest hesitation or searching for a word. Warning: Don't engage him in a contest of repartee . . . you'll lose!

    Once, a lawyer, knowing Chuck was married to a physician asked him (as if that made him an expert in physiology) if a human could live without a spleen. He deadpanned, "Yes, *humans* can, but not lawyers.

    Of course, he gets tit for tat. Since he is known for putting his two cents worth (make that and even dollar) into most debates at the table, another coffee sipper said, "Chuck sure is outspoken."

The lawyer jumped on this one and added, "Really? By whom?"

Back when smoking was still allowed in the restaurant, a smoker pulls out a cigarette and asked (to no one in particular), "Do you mind if I smoke?" Chuck, an ardent non-smoker, responded, "I don't care if you burn!"

Politicians are known to come into City Café during every campaign season. One, who shall remain nameless (primarily because I can't remember who it was) stated he was going to be a pit bull in this campaign. Chuck said dryly, "That's got to have every fire hydrant in Tennessee worried."

+++

Harvell Price

Harvell Price has become a regular at City Café for the past several years since he retired from teaching and being school principal in the West Tennessee Trenton/Milan area. All the waitresses at City just dote on Mr. Price because he brings them presents! I know at least one occasion when he brought them all gifts from Victoria's Secret! His wife says he's harmless, but I don't know . . . He keeps fit by walking the track at Patterson Park nearly every morning after coffee with us. In fact, he's a health nut compared to the rest of us. He orders breakfast most mornings and it consists of one egg, one piece of dry toast, two slices of bacon and a cup of decaf coffee. It's such a regular order for him, they call it the *Harvell*.

He has a hobby of knife making, primarily pen knives. Each is one-of-a-kind by making them different shapes, sizes, and handle materials. The most unusual I've seen to date had ebony wood with a vein of real turquoise running through it. Another was called *The One-Armed Man* knife. It was designed so a man with only one arm could open it . . . and it wasn't a switch blade.

Naturally, Harvell would tell a knife joke at the table. Seems a man was being arraigned for murder. "How do you plead?" asked the Judge. "Not guilty!" the man protested, "The knife slipped!" he added. The judge responded, "Forty-seven times?!!"

+++

Jack Lisi

Jack Lisi is a transplanted Yankee from New York, but despite that, he is a very pleasant fellow. He and his wife, Cheryl, opened a store just off the square called "Let's Make Wine." They sell the equipment and incidental ingredients that enable one to make their own homemade wine and beer.

The Lisi's store began just off East Main on N. Spring St., later moved to the first block of W. Main, and now are operating just a couple of doors from City Café on East Main. So, Jack drops in at City quite often.

In addition to being a Yankee, he's also a Catholic (which softens the Yankee damnation to a tolerable degree) and gives rise to another religious joke. Oddly, the one Jack told manages to offend both Catholic and non-Catholic alike

In a parochial girl's school, one of the nun-teachers asked her students what they wanted to be when they grew up.

The first little girl said, "I want to be a nurse." The nun responded, "A wonderfully helpful occupation!"

The second little girl said, "I want to be a teacher." and the nun replied, "Oh, a very honorable profession!"

The third little girl said, "I want to be a nun like you, Sister." The nun smiled and said, "God bless you, my child!"

The next little girl said, "I want to be a prostitute."

Well, the nun fainted dead away! She laid there on the floor while someone ran to get the Mother Superior.

The elder nun came and revived the sister on the floor. While still lying there, the teacher nun looked up at the last little girl and asked again incredulously, "What did you say you wanted to be?"

The little girl repeated, "A prostitute."

"Oh," sighed the nun, "I thought you said a Protestant!"

+++

Jack Miller

Jack Miller is a retired long-haul truck driver. After 40 years of driving trucks with anything from hot DuPont liquid plastic to automobiles as cargo, he still couldn't get enough of the road, so he took to driving a school bus. It gets him up and going in the morning, he says, and one can tell he really loves those school children. He mentors them and looks after them beyond just picking them up and delivering them. They are lucky kids!

He's also an antique car buff. He has a fully restored 1951 Ford that is completely outfitted as a police car of that era. It's a two-tone black and white, has the search light on the side, the bubble gum machine on top and the police insignia on the sides and back. I guess the only thing that keeps him from being accused of impersonating a police officer is the obvious time warp of the vehicle. Instead, they're liable to call him Barney Fife.

Some of the stories we hear at City involve the storyteller's experiences as a youth. Jack and his wife are from East Tennessee. He went to Seymour High and his wife went just over the hill to Sevierville High. She was in school with Dolly Parton and knew her. Jack says the two girls lived practically next door to one another which, in those parts meant the next hollow (or is it holler?).

Jack and his wife first met as kids, maybe 5 years old, at a church social. She didn't like him much then. (Still doesn't, he jokes, but their 51 years of marriage implies otherwise.)

Having been a Teamster truck driver most of his life, Jack appreciates the story about a fellow that was waiting at the airport for his flight when he noticed a machine sort of like an ATM, but this was back in the '80s before the advent of ATMs. He walked over to it and read the instructions. "Put a quarter in me and I will converse with you."

"Wow, thought the man. I didn't know they had machines that could do that!" So, he put a quarter in and the machine whirred to life.

"What is your I.Q.?" the machine asked.

The man replied, "140."

"And your name?" the machine queried.

"George Abrams." He stated.

"Well, Mr. Abrams, what do you think of . . ." and it went on to talk with the man on a very high intellectual level for about 5 minutes.

When it shut off, the man exclaimed, "My stars! I had no idea we had come so far with computers! I think I'll try it again."

He put another quarter in and the machine whirred to life again.

"What is your I.Q.?" the machine began.

This time the man thought he would have a little experiment with it and replied, "'bout 80, I think."

The machine continued without hesitation, "10-4, Good Buddy, and what's your handle?"

+++

Joe Wolfe

Another of the dearly departed of the many men who have graced the Café is the clothier, Joe Wolfe. For years, he owned and ran a Ladies clothing store on the square. I have just a brief story to tell about Mr. Wolfe. He had gotten old and feeble, but still came in to City on a more-or-less regular basis. It seemed it was all he could do just to get from the doorway to the nearest table where we sat.

I'm proud to say, that compassion sat at that table. When Joe came in, inevitably someone nearest his entry point would jump up and say, "Here, Joe, take my chair." Despite the jokes, the teasing of one another, the feigned offense taken from a good-natured roast of someone at the table, there was a brotherly love present that could touch one's heart.

+++

Jerry Gaither

Jerry Gaither grew up in the Gassaway community of Cannon County and later returned to become a teacher and principal of its school. Subsequently, he worked for the State Education Department, supervising curriculum in several counties of Middle Tennessee. He has been a member of the Rutherford County Board of Commissioners, and even elected superintendent of Rutherford County Schools. I tell you all this so you will realize, if you don't know him, that Jerry is a well-educated, erudite man of many talents. One of which, is pretending to be just a country-bumpkin. Jerry joined us at the community table quite frequently until he moved to Adams Place and had to give up driving.

Once, he put his country-boy persona to use when a stranger sat down at our table who let us know he was a rancher from Texas. Jerry told him he had a little land in Cannon County. The Texan asked how big was his spread? Jerry told him it was just 26 acres, but mighty pretty.

The Texan snorted and bragged, "Why, one time I got in my truck and started driving . . . It took me two days to get from one end of my place to the other!"

Jerry nodded and, in his best country-boy accent, said, "Yup. Had me a truck like that once."

+++

Jerry Benefield

Jerry Benefield led Rutherford County's largest employer during his 12-year tenure as president and CEO of Nissan Motor Manufacturing Corp. USA, and chose to retire here in Murfreesboro.

Around 1980, the Japanese auto company, Nissan, chose Smyrna for its new U.S. plant. Long story short . . . Jerry Benefield ultimately rose to be the president and CEO.

Despite his title and prominence, he remains a down-to-earth friendly fellow that loves to come in and sit with the rest of us at the City Café's community table. Jerry tells this story on himself:

During his 12-year tenure at the helm, it fell to him to host delegations of Japanese executives who came to tour and observe their U.S. plant.

On one such occasion, before Murfreesboro had become a mecca for upscale restaurants, he made reservations to take the Japanese contingent to dinner at a fashionable restaurant in Nashville. He chose the aviation-themed 101st Airborne restaurant adjacent to Nashville's airport, Berry Field.

The 101st Airborne restaurant was built to look like a bombed-out French villa, but was very luxurious inside with many pictures and mementoes showing the nearby Fort Campbell, Kentucky based army unit. There were many photos of bombers and paratrooper planes, and war scenes of WWII in Europe and . . . whoops . . . the Pacific.

Catching Benefield off-guard, what greeted him and the Japanese execs was a bomber plane outside. The Japanese contingent was uneasy with the implication and refused to go in to eat there. It's just as well, because if they had, a picture on the inside lobby of dozens of captured Japanese soldiers with their hands in the air would have greeted them. Jerry smoothed things over by taking them to the nearby New Orleans Manor on Murfreesboro Road. He must be a great diplomat, because he kept his job!

+++

Joel Jobe

Joel Jobe was a CPA with the firm of Jobe, Hastings & Associates. He was a fellow Sunday School class member of mine, another friend who was struck down in the prime of his life. He frequently came to City Café for lunch and related this story about a colleague from another accounting firm who had a funny experience with a neophyte IRS auditor.

It seems his friend, the accountant, accompanied a farmer/client to an IRS audit in Nashville. Seated across from the young and evidently very urban lady auditor, she was going over the farmer's list of deductions when she came to an item labeled "bush hog."

She pounced upon it with an air of "aha," as she squinted over her reading glasses and fired the question, "Tell me, Mr. Smith . . . Did you buy this bush hog for . . . *breeding purposes?*"

The two men laughed so hard and long, the IRS agent, realizing she must have committed an extreme act of naiveté, left the room and got someone else to finish the interview.

For those of you that have the same lack of farm knowledge, a bush hog is a rotary cutting device similar to a lawnmower that is typically pulled behind a tractor and used to cut down brush and heavy weeds in a field.

+++

Bill Cunningham

Bill Cunningham has a wooden leg! At least, it's an artificial limb. How he got it is his story. Bill was raised on a farm near Christiana on the Shelbyville Highway.

He attended the Training School (now called the Homer Pittard Campus School) through 10th grade. That's how far it went in those days (1930s and '40s). Usually, someone in the family brought him to town for school, but occasionally he rode his pony the 8 miles in and tethered it on the school lawn.

For 11th grade, he went to The Webb School, and switched to Columbia Military Academy for his senior year. Then he put that military training to use . . . he joined the army.

When his enlistment was up, he came back to the family farm and had been there only two days when the accident happened.

He was riding on the back of a John Deere tractor that was pulling a bush hog. (Now you see why this particular story is following the previous one.) A farm hand was driving. Bill was steadying himself with one foot on the connecting bar between the tractor and the bush hog.

Suddenly, his pants leg got caught in the power transfer rod that rotates the blades of the mower. Almost instantaneously, it twisted the material and then the flesh of his leg . . . ripped it from the bone!

The farm hand stopped the tractor as quickly as possible, but it was too late. Bill's leg was mangled below the knee beyond repair. The problem now was getting untangled so he could seek medical help.

The farm hand was so shook up he was no help at all. Bill had to take his pocket knife out and cut through the pants and through what was left of the flesh on his lower leg in order to free himself.

His mother called Woodfin's funeral home. No, she wasn't being pessimistic. Back in those days, the funeral homes were the source of ambulances. He was taken to our local Rutherford County Hospital. Doctor's there could not save a limb that had no flesh. They amputated below the knee.

Bill was ultimately fitted for an artificial limb and, to his credit (as if cutting your own flesh away to free yourself isn't credit enough), he learned to walk on it so well that most people don't even realize he has an artificial leg. I had known him for years before I found out.

Bill eventually became a real estate broker with his own company. He developed the fateful farm he inherited into Colonial Estates.

+++

Judge Scott (D.C.) Daniel, Sr.
D.C. (Jim) Daniel, Jr.
Scott Daniel

Judge Scott (D.C.) Daniel, the father of attorneys Jim and Scott Daniel, was a dapper man. He would come into City Café wearing a three-piece suit, watch fob and chain swaging across his vest, and a derby or homburg hat even on the hottest of days. Because his son, Scott was also noted for wearing a nice hat all over town, another Café regular, David Loughry, asked Judge Daniel if the hat du jour was one of Scott's. The Judge took it off, flipped it around to the label and said, "Scott never had a hat this nice!"
Judge Daniel had worked for the National Independent Dairies Association in Washington, D.C. and later as the Secretary and Executive Director of the Federal Trade Commission. He knew personally four presidents, FDR, Truman, Kennedy and LBJ. He had been a federal judge and the title remained the rest of his life like an honorary Kentucky Colonel.

In fact, he was an honorary Mississippi Colonel. Among other important people he had known in Washington was a man who later became governor of Mississippi who invited him down and presented him with the honor.

From him, we heard stories of Washington as it was in the mid-twentieth century, and his earlier life as the proverbial country lawyer.

He told one story about his early law practice when a tenant-farmer-sort asked him to represent him in a criminal case in which he was accused of stealing some chickens. Mr. Daniel asked the man, "Did you steal any chickens?"

"No, sir, Mista Daniel! I didn't steal them chickens!"

"Then I will represent you."

Evidently, he was well represented because, at the conclusion of the trial, he was declared acquitted.

"What do that mean . . . *acquitted*, Mr. Daniel? Do that mean I gotta give them chickens back?"

A similar story was told about the judge when he was hearing a case involving a bootlegger. The defendant was asked his name and he replied, "Joshua, suh."

The judge quickly followed his answer with a whimsical Biblical reference, "Are you the Joshua that made the sun stand still?

"No, suh, Boss!" protested the accused, "I's de Joshua that made the moonshine still."

Judge Daniel addressed many of his acquaintances also as "Judge." His theory was that everybody considers themselves as a judge of something even if it's just whether their hair looks better parted on the right or on the left. (It's also helpful if you can't remember that friend's actual name at the moment!)

Jim Daniel, the eldest son of the judge is another of the many attorneys that City Café served. His specialty was Social Security. He routinely took on the government in his representation of citizens who were trying to get various legitimate benefits that they were being denied. His brother, Scott Daniel, was also an attorney that specialized in . . . well, I'm not sure. He may have done many different kinds of cases, but what I heard more than once was, if you need a good courtroom lawyer, get Scott. Both brothers are retired now, so this doesn't count as an advertisement. Scott didn't come into the café very often, but Jim came frequently up until he had to give up driving because of health reasons.

Jim is probably the most knowledgeable person in Murfreesboro concerning his passion . . . grand opera. He knows the plots, the roles and the famous opera singers. He has a huge collection of opera recordings. If I needed to "Phone a Friend" and the subject was opera, I'd go for double or nothing on Jim. He was an excellent singer, too. He used to sing tenor and did it well enough for soloing with choirs, and special occasions.

With all the attorneys we get at the community table, there is inevitably the latest lawyer joke going around. If it's fresh and funny, the lawyers will laugh along with everyone else. They have a good sense of humor, too. But, it is a drag to hear the same ones over and over, and the lawyer is, of course, always the butt of the joke. However, Jim turned the tables one time with this story:

During a formal dinner at a home in which the hosts had invited several of their friends (some of whom didn't know the other guests, just their hosts), one of the guests started telling the group about a law suit to which they had just recently been involved. Apparently, it had not turned out too favorable for the story teller because he ended it with the pronouncement, "And you know who ended up with all the money . . . THE LAWYERS!"

There was an awkward silence that followed because there was a lawyer and his wife present at the table and everyone except the story teller knew it. Finally, the silence was broken by the lawyer's wife saying, "Oh, I just love a story with a happy ending!"

+++

Larry Sims

Larry Sims is a real estate broker and auctioneer with an office on the square, one of the few offices that isn't occupied by a lawyer or a banker. He knows what's going on in commercial real estate like Rona Barrett knows what's going on in Hollywood gossip. If you want to know what next big thing is coming to the 'boro, ask Larry. He may not tell you, but he'll know.

By the way, Larry has a beautiful wife, Lisa, who is a wonderful artist. Several of the paintings hanging in City Café are hers. She also does sculpturing and has studied with Alan LeQuire, the sculptor of the largest indoor sculpture in the world, the statue of Athena in Nashville's Parthenon. We all kid Larry about having married well above himself.

One day at lunch in City Café, I was sitting at the community table as was Larry. He got up to leave and mentioned that he was headed to an auction of an empty commercial building on South University. He said I ought to come and bid on it. I said I wouldn't buy anything on South University. He cocked his head and said, it's liable to go cheap!

He got my curiosity up. I had nothing better to do that afternoon, so I decided to go and watch the auction. Just watch.

The structure was a concrete block building that was about the size of a four-car garage, if you put two cars in and then pulled two more in behind them. It was an open floor plan except for a small office in the back corner. The office had a big old safe in it; probably weighed about 400 pounds. Other than that, it was pretty much empty except for a little junk. It had been used variously as a beauty parlor and a mechanic's garage with a big garage door to admit vehicles for work. The lot was about 50 x 100. Next door was a small Pentecostal church.

The crowd that showed up for the sale was only about 10 people and they looked to be mostly or entirely neighbors. It was a residential neighborhood.

Larry described the property and the terms (cash within 30 days), Then he asked for a bid to get it started. There was the typical silence from the crowd as everyone waited for someone else to start it.

"Who'll start it off at $20,000? He ambitiously asked. After a few more chants, he dropped his request to $10,000. Nothing. Then he dropped his request for a starting bid to $5,000. Still, no action.

I'm standing there thinking, I don't want this thing, but heck, the lot alone is worth more than $5,000, even if nothing is done but to tear down the building and sell the lot for a Habitat Home. So, I held my hand up, thinking I'll help Larry out and get the bidding started.

Then he chanted the usual, "I have five; who'll make it ten?" After several repetitions, he dropped it to, "Alright, who'll make it $7500?" After touting the virtues of ownership of this fine piece of real estate, he continued, "Who'll make it $6,000?"

There never was another bid. I got it for $5,000. Before giving up on the building and just tearing it down, I did some cleanup of the lot, painted the concrete block exterior (which appeared to have a few bullet hole scars on it), and replaced the leaky roof. Fearful of vandalism on a vacant building, I tried to impress on the neighbors that I was making an effort to do something that would improve their neighborhood. I had a sign company paint a sign that was about 8' x 2' and hung it over the front door. It was a quote I had heard years ago on a religious TV show. "If everyone lit just one little candle, what a bright world this would be." And, you know what? I never had even a scrawl of graffiti while I owned it!

Sometimes, if just one person will fix up and paint up a derelict old house in a run-down area, it will inspire others to do the same and eventually the whole area has become a nice place to live.

After fixing up the property, I rented it out to a plumber as a warehouse for his equipment and supplies. The rent wasn't much, but paid for the insurance, taxes, and minor upkeep. My main goal was to sell it for a profit . . . to "flip it" in real estate parlance.

I listed it at $22,500. Cheap! as Mad Magazine used to say about its price . . . and what Larry Sims had predicted. However, it wasn't snapped up. It stayed on the market over a year, maybe two, before I got an offer of full-price from that little church next door. They were growing and needed expansion room.

The building eventually was torn down for their expansion, but it never did endure any vandalism.

+++

Matthew Royal

Matthew Royal was a deputy sheriff here in Rutherford County and later head of the MTSU campus police department for several years prior to his retirement. Afterwards, he came to City Café most mornings for coffee with the other seniors. He was a fervent NRA advocate and said many times, "If I've got my pants on, I've got my gun."

He could tell a story with a twinkle in his eye that made you know there was going to be a good punch line at its conclusion. Like the time he told us he was interviewing a potential recruit to his department one day and asked him what he would do if he had to arrest his own mother.

The interviewee responded, "Call for backup!"

+++

Mort Cohen

Mort Cohen and his lovely wife, Marilyn owned and operated an interior decorating shop on Church Street adjacent to the WGNS radio station for many years. As a downtown businessman, Mort would occasionally join us at the community table and share stories . . . and jokes. Mort was also an enthusiastic thespian; he acted in many of the plays put on by the Murfreesboro Little Theatre. This penchant was perhaps the reason he could tell a joke so well. The one I remember best told by Mort might be considered a bit "politically incorrect," so I need to preface it with a bit of background.

Firstly, Mort was a proud descendant of God's chosen people . . . he was a Jew. Secondly, I will tell you that I love and respect the Jewish people. I even have a mezuzah mounted on the frame of my front door. If I thought this joke Mort once told at City was a slur on his people, I would not repeat it. But, like Mort, I just think it is funny. In Mort's words:

A Jew was sitting on a park bench and along came a Chinaman who sat down at the other end. Immediately, the Jew started turning red in the face and gritting his teeth until, finally, he hauled off and swatted the Chinaman.

"What was that for?!!" the assaulted one demanded.

"That's for *Pearl Harbor!*" the Jew growled.

"That was the Japanese! I'm Chinese!" protested the oriental.

The unapologetic Jew responded, "*Japanese — Chinese*, same difference!"

Well, the Chinaman just sat there and got madder and madder until he turned and swatted the Jew with equal force.

"What was that for?" stammered the Jew.

"That's for sinking the *Titanic!*" the Chinaman smugly replied.

"What do you mean, 'Sinking the Titanic?' An iceberg sunk the Titanic!"

The Chinaman smiled and said, "*Iceberg — Goldberg*, same difference!"

+++

Herschel Mullins
Charles Mullins (the jeweler)

Mullins Jewelers was on the south side of the square (almost next door to where City Café began) for 69 years, finally closing in 2007. But the founder, Herschel, was blessed to live until 2012 (age 96), long enough to see his legacy continue through grandson, Jeff Mullins who opened J.Mullins, Jewelers in 2010.

Herschel was trained as a watchmaker and served as an aircraft instrument repairman at Sky Harbor and Sewart Air Base during WWII.

It is such a blessing to go into a so-called Mom & Pop business and see family members working together. I remember seeing 4 generations at once in the Mullins Jewelers on the square. Herschel was, by then, in his 80s but still working and, though he had thick glasses, he could swing those goggle-eyed jeweler's specs over them and still manipulate the most delicate of inner works in a watch. Charlie, his son, was in his 60s and did the general management. Granddaughter, Kathy, was minding the counter, and her toddler was quietly playing with a toy in a corner.

The family reminded me of the Dutch author Corrie ten Boom and how she described her father's watch shop in Haarlem, Holland. The family lived above the shop and consequently she and her siblings grew up in the same setting. Corrie's most famous book is *The Hiding Place* which describes her Christian family's efforts to hide their Jewish neighbors in their attic (much the same as was portrayed in *The Diary of Anne Frank*) during the Nazi occupation.

Corrie ten Boom wrote several other books inspired by her devout Christian father. One of them, *In My Father's House*, portrayed growing up in the watch shop. I once gave a copy of this book to Charlie Mullins because his family business reminded me so much of Corrie's descriptions of her family.

I know I'm digressing again here, but it's my book and I can write whatever I want! And, right now, what I want is to give you, dear Reader, a taste of Corrie ten Boom's writing, now that I am reminded of it. Here's an excerpt from one of her sequel to *The Hiding Place*. I trust it is brief enough to be considered, with all due acknowledgement, fair use:

> We were going to see one of the many poor families in the neighborhood whom Mama had adopted. It never occurred to any of us children that we ourselves were poor; "the poor" were people you took baskets to. Mama was always cooking up nourishing broths and porridges for forgotten old men and pale young mothers--on days, that is, when she herself was strong enough to stand at the stove.
> The night before, a baby had died, and with a basket of her own fresh bread Mama was making the prescribed call on the family. She toiled painfully up the rail less stairs, stopping often for breath. At the top a door opened into a single room that was obviously cooking,

eating, and sleeping quarters all at once. There were already many visitors, most of them standing for lack of chairs. Mama went at once to the young mother, but I stood frozen on the threshold. Just to the right of the door, so still in the homemade crib, was the baby.

It was strange that a society which hid the facts of sex from children made no effort to shield them from death. I stood staring at the tiny unmoving form with my heart thudding strangely against my ribs. Nollie [my sister], always braver than I, stretched out her hand and touched the ivory-white cheek. I longed to do it too, but hung back, afraid. For a while curiosity and terror struggled in me. At last I put one finger on the small curled hand.

It was cold.

Cold as we walked back to the Beje, cold as I washed for supper, cold even in the snug gas-lit dining room. Between me and each familiar face around the table crept those small icy fingers. For all Tante Jans's talk about it, death had been only a word. Now I knew that it could really happen--if to the baby, then to Mama, to Father, to Betsie!

Still shivering with that cold, I followed Nollie up to our room and crept into bed beside her. At last we heard Father's footsteps winding up the stairs. It was the best moment in every day, when he came up to tuck us in. We never fell asleep until he had arranged the blankets in his special way and laid his hand for a moment on each head. Then we tried not to move even a toe.

But that night as he stepped through the door I burst into tears. "I need you!" I sobbed. "You can't die! You can't!"

Beside me on the bed Nollie sat up. "We went to see Mrs. Hoog," she explained. "Corrie didn't eat her supper or anything."

Father sat down on the edge of the narrow bed. "Corrie," he began gently, "when you and I go to

Amsterdam...when do I give you your ticket?"

I sniffed a few times, considering this.

"Why, just before we get on the train."

"Exactly. And our wise Father in heaven knows when we're going to need things, too. Don't run out ahead of Him, Corrie. When the time comes that some of us will have to die, you will look into your heart and find the strength you need...just in time."

(Excerpted from Tramp for the Lord, by Corrie ten Boom with Jamie Buckingham; Published by Christian Literature Crusade, Fort Washington, Pennsylvania and Fleming H. Revell Company, Old Tappan, New Jersey)

Now, Reader, take your time, and when you are ready, let me continue with the story of the Mullins.

Herschel and Charlie used to frequent City Café, but as age slowed Herschel down, it was just Charlie that we would see. Having already taken up more space with this family than any other entry, I'll just tell a brief story of Charlie's with, as you will soon see, an apropos subject.

Three Russian's were in the former communist state's prison back when worker morale was at its lowest. Production volume and quality were at an all-time low. The men got to talking about what got them in prison.

The first prisoner said he came to work early and was accused of being a spy.

The second said he came to work late and was accused of being a traitor.

The third said he came to work on time . . . and was accused of buying a foreign watch!

+++

Charles Mullins (the preacher)
Randall Chaudoin
Jim Avaritt

You know the Holy Trinity, but do you know the Unholy Trinity? That would be these three preachers that would sit together at the round table in the mornings and think up zingers on each other.

Randall Chaudoin, until his passing in 2006, was a regular at City Café. He was an educator, having served as principal at Hobgood Elementary and Middle Tennessee Christian School, and a gospel preacher of the Church of Christ faith. He was a witty man that liked to kid with his friends and could take a tease as well as he could give one.

Once, while recuperating in the hospital, someone called his room to inquire how he was getting along. Disguising his voice, Randall himself answered sadly, "I'm sorry, but Mr. Chaudoin passed away two hours ago. Jennings & Ayers funeral home has already picked up the remains." This lie was reported at the East Main Church of Christ on Sunday, upsetting the whole congregation.

His friend and fellow C of C preacher, Charles Mullins, who is also a regular morning coffee drinker at City, once picked Randall up from a hospital in Birmingham to bring him home to Murfreesboro. Stopping at a Cracker Barrel restaurant en route, Randall inquired about the special of the day. The waitress, after giving the usual response, added that they had some left-over meatloaf from yesterday that was better. Randall acted shocked that the waitress would push yesterday's leftovers instead of the special of the day and said, "Miss, do you know who this is? (Gesturing toward Charles) This is Mr. Dan Evans (founder and CEO of the Cracker Barrel chain).

Charles played along. The waitress quickly disappeared into the kitchen, fearful she was about to lose her job for her frankness. I'm sure the two preachers did the Christian thing and told her they were just kidding. Or did they?

Jim Avaritt, the Baptist preacher, and Mullins were doing their regular visitation at the hospital one day when Charles noticed Jim had parked in the space reserved for the anesthesiologist. Charles chastised him for this, but Rev. Avaritt responded it was all right because he had put more people to sleep than the doctor.

Jim told one on himself with the story of a little boy who brought him his piggy bank. "Why are you giving this to me, son?" Rev. Avaritt asked.

" 'cause my Mama and Daddy said you was the poorest preacher they had ever seen!"

One time Bro. Avaritt announced to his congregation: "I have good news and bad news. The good news is, we have enough money to pay for our new building program. The bad news is, it's still out there in your pockets."

Randall said, "A liberal member of the Church of Christ is one that thinks a Baptist is going to heaven."

Randall complained one day that he wasn't going back to that school (referring to where he was principal) until they took back what they said to him. Charles asked what they had said. "You're fired!" replied Randall.

This writer got a chance to tease Randall one day when the table discussion had turned to the Church of Christ ban against musical instruments in the church service. I declared that, "Randall, here, says that 'When the Lord comes back to the sound of the trumpet, He better not play it in MY church!'"

Randall took a lot of kidding about his ultra-conservative denominational views, a fair amount of which came from J.D. Kennedy, a friend of both Randall and fellow Campbellite, Charles Mullins. Once in the café, Randall smiled at J.D.'s teasing appreciation of deigning to even speak to a Methodist, and fired back, "Just because you're going to Hell, J.D., doesn't mean I can't be nice to you.

Randall once said there were 200 restaurants in Murfreesboro and yet he still comes in here to get insulted.

A similar story involves all three of the aforementioned. Charles Mullins, the Church of Christ preacher got up from the table with an almost empty glass of water. Randall asked where he was going and Charles replied, "I'm going to baptize all the Methodists in Murfreesboro. Methodist, J.D. Kennedy, sitting at the same table, interjected, "Charles! I'm hurt!"

Charles, fearing he had actually insulted his friend, apologized for the reference to the Methodists' ritual of sprinkling for a baptism. J.D. then added, "No, it's not that. I'm hurt because when Gabriel blows his horn, you won't recognize the sound and won't get to go!"

Once, at the preacher's table, I was lamenting the split my church was going through. Bro. Jim Avaritt told me a story about a man who had been discovered living on a deserted island as a castaway for several years. When they sent a rowboat from the ship to pick him up, the rescuers saw three grass huts he had built on the island. They asked him what the three huts were used for and he replied,

"Well, this one here is my home; it's the one I live in. That one over there is my church; it's where I worship."

Not hearing an explanation for the third one, they pointed to it and asked its purpose.

"Hmph! the castaway sneered. That's where I used to go to church."

+++

J.D. Kennedy

J.D. Kennedy was a graduate of the Air Force Academy in Colorado Springs. Following graduation, he was a pilot in Viet Nam. He'll quickly add, "Not a fighter pilot; I flew cargo planes." J.D. asks, "How can you tell when a fighter pilot comes into the room?" . . . "He'll tell you!"

J.D. loves to tell academy stories and told one about a cadet that got a little too enthusiastic about the first Colorado snow of the season. He opened his barracks window, scraped together some snow on the outer sill and formed it into a snowball. He couldn't resist throwing it at the first target he saw. That target turned out to be a faculty officer who got hit squarely in the back of the neck.

As the officer turned around to see where the missile had come from, the cadet, realizing what his still boyish impulse had done, slammed the window shut and watched in trepidation as the officer headed for his barracks door.

The officer burst in and found about a dozen cadets, all dressed alike and looking as much like the assailant as his brief glance had managed to record.

Figuring that the culprit would have cold hands from having just made a snowball, he ordered all the cadets to hold out their hands as he methodically felt of each pair.

No one had cold hands. Then he noticed a sliding door that closed on a closet where gear was stored. He walked over to it and slid it open. There stood a scared and shivering cadet with hands down at his side.

There was a moment of silence and then the cadet said, "Going down, Sir?"

J.D. also tells a spurious story about an officer that called the motor pool wanting to get something he could drive into town. He asked the E-2 what vehicles were available that day.

The equivalent of a PFC answered, "Well, we got two jeeps, a four-ton truck, an amphibious vehicle and, oh yeah, we got one limo for the fat-assed colonels around here."

The officer was shocked. "Airman! Do you know who you're speaking to?"

"Uh, no sir." Replied the brash kid.

"This is COLONEL James Hutcheson!"

The motor pool lackey replied, "Uh, Colonel, do you know who you are talking to?"

"No, who is it?"

Hanging up the phone, the last words the colonel heard were, "Bye, fat-ass."

+++

Robert Holt

Robert Holt is originally from Milan, Tennessee. He's one of those guys you'd like to slap silly because he's your age, but looks 20 years younger. Actually, he is about 10 years younger than I am, but has enough knowledge to be 10 years older. It's odd how we think alike. When someone else at our table says something, we both come out with the same comment at the same time. We even look at each other and smile when someone else says something, and know we're thinking the same thing that hasn't occurred to anyone else.

Robert, who is not a "Bob," though Truman Jones insists on calling him that just to tease him, is full of stories and they are always interesting, partly because he tells them so well, and usually has a grin on his face that makes you wonder what's coming next.

He told of a cousin of his, Danny Mulally, who is currently director of golf at Golf Club of the Everglades near Naples, Florida. Danny was working as a golf pro at Marko Island and was playing a round with the famous golf legend Gene Sarazen.

Sarazen noticed a special tag hanging on Mulally's golf bag and asked him what it was. Danny explained that while he was playing in a tournament for Bethel College in McKenzie, Tennessee, he made a double eagle on one of the holes. (Some call it an Albatross. It's the rarest of golf shots, even more so than a hole-in-one; it's finishing a hole with a three-under-par. Only way to do it is shooting a 2 on a par-5, or a hole-in-one on a par 4.) The magazine, Golf Digest, gave him the tag as an acknowledgement and memento of the feat.

Danny Mulally proudly went into some detail describing the occasion to the famous Sarazen. "After my initial drive, I cut the corner on what was supposed to be a dog-leg and went straight for the green. I hit a 5-iron and, lo and behold, it went into the cup!"

Gene Sarazen smiled and said, "I hit a double-eagle once." That's all he said. But the next day a courier arrived at Danny's door bearing a gift from Gene. Unwrapping it, he found it was a signed print of a newspaper sports page with Sarazen's picture and the story titled, "Shot heard round the world!"

Turned out, that shot was made on the Sunday final in the 1935 Master's Tournament at the famous par-5 "Amen Corner." It tied him for the lead which he went on to win for the championship of the most prestigious golf tournament in America.

No less an authority than Murfreesboro's own Grantland Rice, America's first great sports writer and a founding member of Augusta National, called it "... the most thrilling single golf shot ever played."

"I hit a double-eagle once." What an understatement!

+++

Truman Jones

Truman Jones, as mentioned earlier, is a former Rutherford County Sheriff. Nowadays, he has a radio program cleverly titled "The Truman Show." Oh, that's been mentioned previously, too. Well, I guess there isn't much left to be said about Truman.

Oh, yeah. He's impressed with my recital of Kipling's *Gunga Din*. Somehow, I was prodded into reciting all 5 minutes of it in pseudo-Cockney British accent. Afterwards, I asked him what he thought of my execution. He said he was in favor of it.

Anyway, he's goaded me into repeating the whole thing two or three times when other friends of his were in the restaurant. That's one of his talents. He can talk other people into doing things. That's how he fills the talk show with variety and interest. Of course, he has a Plan B. If no one of interest shows up for his on air dialogue, he calls his buddy, Avent (see above . . . again).

Sometimes their banter gets a bit like Abbott and Costello. One time, Avent said to Truman, "You are showing a great deal of contempt for me!"

Truman apologized, saying, "Sorry, I was trying to hide it."

+++

Ron Williams

    Ron Williams has been a store owner, a farmer, and a county commissioner. He comes into City quite often and nearly always has a tale to tell.
    One morning, he ordered a bowl of grits at the café. When they came, he just sat there staring at them. Then he said to the waitress, "Taste those grits."
    "Why, is something wrong with them?"
    "Just taste them!" Ron insisted.
    She looked around the table and then said, "Where's your spoon?"
    "Aha!" Ron replied . . . making his point the subtle way.

    Ron had a business for 20-some-odd years on Nashville's Broadway between First and Second Avenue. He sold antiques and miscellaneous trinkets, but said he made his best money on pages torn out of old magazines.
    Traveling around to flea markets and such in search of antiques for his inventory, he noticed that some vendors were selling old magazines . . . *Life, Look, Saturday Evening Post,* etc. They got about a dollar apiece for them. Then he noticed some other vendors

were selling what they call "tear sheets," just a single sheet torn out of a magazine. These usually featured an ad for things such as Coca-Cola, old cars, anything nostalgic. These sellers were getting as much or more for a single page of the right thing as the others were getting for the entire magazine.

    He asked the magazine sellers why they didn't sell by the page the good stuff. Responses were like, "Aw, I don't have time to go digging through these old magazines for special stuff."

    Ron saw a gold mine. He started buying old magazines, tearing out the interesting ads and categorizing them for easy retrieving. He even bought a device for cutting mattes so he could matte and shrink wrap the pages. He said he had about 58 cents in the entire matted pages and sold them for $7.95 each . . . until someone told him he was selling them too cheap! He upped the price to $20 each and tripled his sales. "Value is a perceived thing that has nothing to do with cost!" he learned.

    He started buying collections of magazines and eventually had what he believes was the largest collection perhaps in the world. He had over a million magazines in that 5000 square foot store on Broadway. He was selling to walk-in customers and to museums, manufacturers who were now collecting old ads of their products, and retailers.

The Cracker Barrel restaurant chain agreed to give his matted, shrink-wrapped old ads a trial run in 10 of their stores. Ron said he placed an assortment in each of the 10 stores and then made trips back to them to surreptitiously buy back his own product. He was going to make sure the trial was a success. (Nothing in their agreement said he couldn't!) The trial was a success and he sold hundreds to Cracker Barrel who did well with the nostalgic ephemera themselves.

This was all before the internet and eBay were big factors in reselling. Ron saw the handwriting on the wall and sold out his business before he had to start competing with every small operator with a couple of old magazines.

+++

Dan Austin
Harold Nipper
Dave Robertson

Dan Austin was co-owner and co-broker with Harold Nipper of Austin & Nipper Century 21 Real Estate Office back in 1980 when I first got my start in real estate with their firm. The partnership broke up amicably in 1981. Dan later became my broker again when he became the broker of record for the Bob Parks office in which I spent a very satisfying 24 years.

    During a lunch at City, Dan relayed the story of Harold and another well-known Realtor of that era, Dave Robertson. The two had formed a venture partnership to develop some land out Sulphur Springs Road into a small subdivision. They were taking their banker (who shall remain nameless) to see the progress of the development after the grading for the streets had been completed...

    Harold and Dave were in the front seat of the car; the banker was in the back. As they turned off Sulphur Springs Road onto the freshly graded main road of the subdivision, Harold explained that they were going to name this street *Timberland Drive.*

    When they came to an intersecting cross street, he added, "And this street is going to be named *Ruby Dr.*

    "Ruby?!!" blurted the banker. "Why would you name a street Ruby? Sounds like an old French whore's name!"

Harold slammed on the brakes, turned to the back seat and with eyes narrowed said, "Happens to be my mother's name!"

Dave, who had whipped his head around, too, added coldly, "Happens to be MY mother's name, too!"

Today, one can verify at least part of this story by looking at a Rutherford county map and finding Timberlake Drive running off Sulphur Springs Rd. just before the latter goes under State Route 840. The map will also show a cross street with the name of Ruby Drive. Both Harold and Dave regrettably passed away still in their prime. Their obituaries did indeed reveal that they both had mothers with the beautiful name of *Ruby*.

+++

Tom Brown

I have to be careful or I will write too much about Tom Brown, a man I count among my most admired. He was one of the most sincere and active (not passive) Christians I have ever known. He was a deacon at First Baptist Church, patriarch to a large family, all of whom followed in his footsteps and grew up to be faithful servants of God. See there, I've already gone to pontificating.

Tom passed away recently at the age of 90. For the past several years he had been taking many of his meals at City Café. His children donated the bench that sits out in front of the café in his honor, and we who knew him and saw him sitting either inside or out there so frequently are delighted to have that remembrance.

I wrote an earlier book entitled *Universal Rx: The Hug*. It was a book of poems, essays and short stories each of which had an illustration. One of them used Tom for the illustration. I took a photo of Tom sitting at a booth (when City Café still had booths) eating his meal, and gave it to my illustrator who drew an excellent likeness for the book.

The story described an old man sitting alone in a restaurant overhearing the squeals, chatter, cries, and protestations of an infant whose parents were trying to have a quiet meal. Many in the restaurant cast annoyed glances at the child, but the old man just sat and remember the past when it might have been one of his children inconsolably distraught in a public place. Or even earlier when he might have been the guilty infant himself. A slight smile comes to the old man's face in his reverie, and a tear attests the sanctity of that remembrance.

The noisy infant's father stops by the old man's table as they are leaving and apologizes for the aggravation of his child during the meal. The old man looks up and responds, "You might as well apologize for the robin's song." That was Tom Brown.

The only story I can remember Tom telling in City was a brief one that I suspect was an adaptation of a joke. Tom's late wife's name was Helen. She lost a battle with cancer several years earlier. She was as dedicated as he to Christian living, so she probably didn't really say what I'm about to repeat. But, in defense of both of them, even Christians have a sense of humor.

Tom said a man came up to Helen one time and said, "You look like Helen Brown." And she responded, "Well, you don't look so hot in blue yourself!"

+++

Tom Haynes
Johnny Jones

Tom Haynes is considered to be one of the premier real estate attorneys in Murfreesboro. I did a lot of closings with him when I was a real estate agent. He also frequents City Café. Tom's family is old Murfreesboro. He grew up here, but attended school at Castle Heights Military Academy in Lebanon.

He once told the story of a time when he and Johnny Jones (who was also old Murfreesboro and a real estate broker . . . not John Jones, real estate broker (that's his very successful son).

Tom and Johnny had the day off at Castle Heights. They were not supposed to go off campus but could roam the campus without supervision as long as they were back in their rooms for taps at 10 PM. However, the two took off for Murfreesboro. Once here, they split up with the agreement to meet at Murfreesboro's Tops drive-in restaurant at 9 PM so Johnny could ride back to Lebanon with Tom.

Tom waited at the appointed hour and place, but no Johnny. He waited until 9:15; still no Johnny. He waited until 9:30; still no Johnny. He couldn't wait any longer and took off in his dad's 1960 T-bird (this was in 1962). Tom claims he made it all the way to the square in Lebanon in 13 minutes!

Unfortunately, that still wasn't fast enough to get all the way to the campus, park the car and get to his dorm room. He was just a few minutes late, and received a few demerits, but it wasn't enough to have to walk the bull ring.

Johnny, however, finally got there at 4 AM the next morning. He tried to sneak in, but was caught and received 50 demerits and loss of rank. This was his senior year. Tom says that Johnny couldn't finish walking off all his demerits by the end of the school term and had to stay after to finish them so he could get his diploma.

+++

John Parker

John Parker is the owner and operator of Middle Tennessee Coin & Jewelry, Inc. The shop used to be located on Maple St. behind what used to be Murfreesboro Bank & Trust. (Seems the older I get, the more that phrase "used to be" creeps into my conversation.) If you were ever in the store, you would remember a huge aquarium with lots of multi-colored coral and bright tropical fish.

Ever since the county took over all the Maple St. buildings adjacent to the judicial building, John has been located on the top floor of the Sun Trust building on East Main. From either location, City Café was a conveniently short walk that he made and continues frequently to make for lunch.

When I told Parker the story at City about dropping someone's golf ball in the cup then hightailing it so they would think they had made a hole-in-one, John one-upped me with this story.

He was playing in a night tournament at Stones River Country Club. Participants are given a ball that glows so they can follow it as it flies through the night air. This was a scramble in which teams of 4 players are matched up so that each team had an A, B, C, and D player. The A player is a good player with a low handicap. The D player is the weakest. John was the A player, one of the ladies was an avid golfer and the other woman was a beginner. The way the scramble works is that each player hits a drive from the tee box. Then the best shot is chosen, the other three balls are collected and they all play their second shot from the location of the best first shot. The same happens with each succeeding shot.

Then they came to a par-3. Two of the initial shots were unusable, then John hit his tee-shot. It seemed the right direction and the right distance as best their eyes could tell in the darkness. But, it disappeared. Could have rolled off the back of the elevated green to where it couldn't be seen. Or . . .

dare he hope . . . gone in the cup? He had to wait to find out though while the ladies hit their tee-shots from the ladies' tee.

Lo, and behold, the experienced lady's ball disappeared in the same manner! Finally, they walked over to the green and, sure enough, found a glow coming out of the hole . . . but only one ball. Whose ball was it? The woman, or the A player, neither of whom had ever had a hole-in-one? There ensued some potential hard feelings over the ownership of the ace, especially from the lady's husband.

As fortune would have it, a non-player who happened to be near enough to see the feat walked up and explained it was not either of the last two balls hit, it was the earlier one from the men's tee. That meant John, after years of effort, had his coveted hole-in-one!

Now, there is a tradition that when a player scores a hole-in-one, he treats everyone in the clubhouse to a round of drinks. That night, partly because of the tournament, there were quite a few in the clubhouse. John's tab for the treat ran to a shocking $200.00!

However, it also came as a shock to that observer-fellow who witnessed the event. You see, that guy had the same warped sense of humor that I have. John's ball hadn't disappeared into the cup. It had disappeared into that man's hand, who had quickly run over and deposited it in the cup.

Evidently, he was a jokester with a conscience. He might have let John go to his grave thinking he had made that hole-in-one, but he couldn't let John get stuck with that huge bar bill. He came up to John and explained that his prank was meant for someone else. In the darkness, he thought it was his friend that had hit the ball. When John's group showed up at the green, he just played out his joke on John, not thinking about the 19th -hole celebration. He told John he would cover the bar tab.

True to his word, the next business day, he paid off the bar's bill . . . all in cash. (He didn't want to have to explain a check to his wife.)

John's still hunting for that first ace.

P.S. Just before sending this manuscript to the printers, I discovered in a visit to my dental hygienist, Carolyn Burgin at Dr. Jim Bishop's office, that she was the "novice woman golfer" in the above story! Our small town is getting bigger, but it's still a small world.

+++

Karon Robinson
Sharon Matheny

Sharon Matheny and twin sister Karon Robinson have been daily customers at City for the last several years after retiring. Even in retirement age, the identical twins are hard to tell apart. Sharon retired from the Tennessee Bureau of Investigation, and Karon, from teaching and assistant principal of Riverdale High School.

These two girls aren't at all intimidated by a table full of old men. When they first started coming in, they walked over, introduced themselves and asked if we minded if they joined us at the table. We didn't mind at all adding a little class to the table.

Sharon told a story about her trip with her family to Hawaii. This was a trip with her parents, twin Karon and other family members when she was 25 years old and still unmarried.

Every afternoon about 1 or 2 PM, a high school band would parade down the main street near where they were staying on Oahu Island. When it got to a little park, it would stop and play a concert.

One day, she followed the band to the park and stood there as they played a jazzy arrangement that got her to swaying and nodding with the beat. A group of 5 Navy boys were sitting on a blanket nearby and invited her to share it with them and have a seat. I told you she wasn't the shy type, so she joined them just like she did our table full of men.

After the concert, the sailors offered to show her around the island. Again, she took them up on it. Their means of transportation was the bus line that served the island like a metropolitan bus line does for a city. They went all over the island and, by 10 PM were on the far side of the island where the boys had an apartment. They were about to put her on the bus to send her back to her family's location when they discovered the bus route had ceased running for the night. (Don't you wonder if those sailors didn't know the schedule well? Was this the Hawaiian equivalent of running out of gas on a date?)

They offered to let her spend the night at their apartment, and, well, she was 25 and felt she could take care of herself. She called Karon and told her the situation. She told Karon to tell their parents that she was feeling a little fatigued and had gone to her room to sleep, and to please not waken her.

Well, Sharon spent the night with 5 young sailors and she says not a one of them made the slightest improper move toward her. (Kinda destroys your image of sailors, don't it?)

She caught the first bus back to the other side of the island the next morning and the parents were never the wiser. Karon never told on her. Either Karon is a sweet and loyal sister, or Sharon's got enough on her twin to guarantee mutual secrecy.

Karon's story sounds like something out of the Christmas Story (No, not the one in Mark and Luke; the one about the little boy with the Holy Grail of Christmas presents, an official, Model 1938, Daisy Red Ryder BB gun. "You'll shoot your eye out with that thing, kid!")

In Karon's case it was a toy shovel. This one had a wooden handle and a metal scoop. She wasn't using it to shovel, though. She was using it to bust into a tool shed they had in the back yard.

She was about 6 years old and wasn't supposed to get into that shed. But, clever Karon was using the shovel to extend her reach to the latch on its door. She was trying to pry the latch open when the metal scoop broke off of the handle. The scoop dropped smack into her face and cut it just beside her right eye, barely missing the eyeball.

She was doing something she wasn't supposed to be doing, broke her toy, and nearly put her eye out. What was she going to tell her mother?

It so happened that while she was trying to do her breaking and entering, her mother was nearby mowing the grass in their dog's pen. Mother was always complaining about the chewed up bones that littered the pen. It was hard to cut grass without the mower picking up bones and hurling them around.

"Aha!" thought the little miscreant. I'll tell her that one of those bones she was throwing hit me and nearly put my eye out!

The ploy worked just as sweetly as it did for Ralphie and the icicle. Not until over 50 years later did Karon 'fess up and tell her mother what had really happened.

"What?!" her mother, exclaimed. "You let me think all these years that I had nearly blinded my child!"

+++

B.B. Gracy, III

Speaking of BBs, I'll mention a long-time beloved customer, B.B. Gracy.

B.B. was the son of one of the early faculty members of Middle Tennessee Normal. I know this because I had an aunt who attended Normal and she dated B.B. Gracy, II, who was a coach and teacher there. This was, of course, before he married and produced the subject of this heading.

B.B. (III) lived right across from the school's gymnasium on Middle Tennessee Boulevard virtually all his life. He retired as Clerk and Master of the Chancery Court, so he was in the antebellum courthouse on the square for many years.

As a paraplegic, he could not readily get up and down the stairs in the years prior to an elevator being installed. He would order a lunch from City Café and it would be brought to him. When the courthouse finally got an elevator (albeit, the slowest vertical mode of transportation outside of sitting on a tree and waiting for it to grow) he began rolling himself in his wheelchair to the café.

Garry Simpson remembers B.B. always had a positive attitude and was, "the most gracious guy in a wheelchair I ever knew."

B.B. asked once for a bigger hamburger than the standard size Garry served. To accommodate him, Garry created a big burger that he named after B. B. Afterwards, many patrons would ask for a BB Special Burger.

+++

Henry Lane

Henry Lane was a state trooper and member of the 10 O'clock Coffee Club of City Café. I wasn't a member of that elite group, so I didn't get to converse with him much, but he occasionally came in at other times and sat at the community table. The one story I remember him telling was told laughingly about an unnamed colleague of his.

Trooper Lane said that a member of his highway patrol office pulled over a young lady for speeding and asked to see her driver's license. The girl complied and handed him her license. He looked at it and then back at her and said accusingly, "Says here, you're supposed to be wearing glasses!"

"But, officer, the sweet-young-thing retorted, "I have contacts!" batting her eyelashes at him.

The patrolman shot back indignantly, "Well, I don't care *WHO* you know!"

+++

Randy Smotherman

It's been said that no one is considered a real Murfreesboroan unless they were born and bred here.

(Isn't that expressions backwards? Shouldn't it be *bred and born*?) Randy Smotherman is a home-grown fellow, but he attended school at Franklin's Battle Ground Academy, so other locals consider him somewhat suspect.

Randy owns and operates an antique store. He's got as much junk, I mean fine old heirlooms, as many antique malls with dozens of dealers. He really does have a fascinating assortment of vintage items! Look him up on the internet.

Anyway, Randy tells the story of an antique dealer on the boardwalk at Atlantic City that had among his wares a small bronze figurine of a rat.

A visitor browsing in the store was attracted to it for some reason and asked how much it was. The dealer said, "$50 for the statuette and $200 for the story."

The customer raised an eyebrow at the odd option, but said, "Just sell me the bronze." He paid the $50 and walked out with the figure.

Soon, he noticed there were a couple of real rats following him. As he rounded a corner, more rats joined them. Within a couple of blocks there were dozens joining the pack, then hundreds, then thousands!

The man was getting so nervous he turned onto one of the piers that jut out into the ocean, walked to the end of it and threw the effigy into the ocean.

The rats raced to the edge of the pier and jumped in after it, committing suicide like the lemmings of Norway that stampede over the cliffs.

The man returned to the antique store where he had bought the bronze. The dealer laughed and said, "So, you're back for the story, aren't you!"

"No," the man replied, "I came back to see if you had a little bronze of a lawyer?"

+++

John Farmer

John Farmer is a retired station manager for Delta Airlines. He's also a golfing buddy of mine, a deacon at my church and a devoted husband about to celebrate his golden wedding anniversary with wife, Sue, whom he nearly always brings when he comes to City Café. All this makes him sound a lot better than he deserves, so forget I said it.

Anyway, our preacher (a really good one!), Dr. Noel Schoonmaker, announced in the pulpit that, with the 2016 Olympics about to begin in Rio, he was going to be preaching on athletic metaphors in the Bible the next Sunday. That put John in mind of this football story which he couldn't wait to tell at the next visit to City.

John told a story he heard from the well-known motivational speaker, John Cassis, about a locker room pep talk that Mike Ditka gave his Chicago Bears just before going out on the field. Cassis was serving as Chaplain for the Bears during their 1980s glory days.

Ditka told the team that he had something to say to them. Looking around and spotting William "Refrigerator" Perry (who could miss the big defensive tackle's hulking 330 pounds?), Ditka added that when he was finished he wanted William to close with the Lord's Prayer.

Immediately, the Fridge got that deer caught in the headlights look. He started sweating and looking around while Ditka continued his pep talk.

Quarterback Jim McMahon elbowed Cassis and whispered, "Look at Perry! He doesn't know the Lord's Prayer. I'll bet 50 bucks he doesn't know it!" Cassis thought, "Everybody knows the Lord's Prayer." (Back in Perry's school days of the 60's, it was still recited in many schools at the beginning of every day.) Cassis, being the optimist he was, said he'd take that bet. (No mention of the irony of gambling on a sacred text!)

When Ditka finished his speech, he nodded to the Fridge. There was an awkward moment of silence, but finally William Perry began, "Now I lay me down to sleep, I pray the Lord my soul to keep . . ."

While this continued, McMahon whispered to Cassis, "Well, I'll be danged! I didn't think he would know it!"

+++

Drs. David & Lorraine Singer

Both David and Lorraine Singer have PhDs and taught until retirement at MTSU. Lorraine also taught at the Homer Pittard Campus School part of the time. Imagine having a person with a PhD as a teacher for your kindergartener! Such is the strong possibility when you are lucky enough to get your child into the Campus School as were my wife and I.

Lorraine tells of one of her college students who had to miss a test. She received a call early one morning before the class that went like this:

"Dr. Singer, I'm calling on behalf of Mary Smith who is in your 9 AM class. She asked me to tell you she was sick and unable to attend the class and will have to miss the test today."

"Oh, I'm so sorry to hear that." Lorraine replied. "I do hope it's not serious. And who is this calling?"

"Uh . . . this is my roommate."

David remembers a time in the early '70s when a fellow named André worked as a bus boy at City Café. He was actually an inmate at the local jail, but they let him out to work during the day. He only had a 30-day sentence to serve, but he kept skipping out around the 28th day. They'd recapture him and add a month to his sentence then, oddly enough, continue letting him out during the day to continue working at the café.

Shortly before that sentence was fully served, he'd do it again. David thinks he was just a homeless fellow that did it to have a warm, safe place to sleep at night. Eventually, he disappeared for good. I suppose the moral of this story is everybody's got a story.

+++

Marvin Briley

Marvin Briley was a long-time Murfreesboro plumber. At one time, his was the largest plumbing company in the city. By the '90s, Marvin's son, Buddy, had pretty much taken over the day-to-day management and Marvin was free to come to City Café every morning.

He would order the same thing nearly every day . . . a couple of biscuits and ask for butter and the honey bear. He had what is, to me, a strange ritual of putting the butter on his plate, blending in the honey until he had a homogenous slurry. Then he would hold his biscuit, slather a knife full of the mixture on the edge and take a bite. He would repeat this routine with each succeeding bite until all biscuits and honey-butter had been consumed. I never understood why he didn't just open the biscuit and spread the concoction all at once. I have noticed other people eat biscuits that way, too, but still don't understand the logic.

Marvin told the story of a doctor calling him in the middle of the night with a clogged toilet. Marvin told him to drop two aspirins in it and if it wasn't better in the morning to call him back.

By the way, Marvin never got out of the 1940s when it came to leaving a tip for the waitress. He was notorious for leaving just a dime. I don't think it was because he was cheap or didn't like the service. He was just taught when he was a kid that you leave a dime tip for an order of two biscuits and honey.

+++

Bill Shacklett
Richard (Dick) Shacklett

Richard and Ginny Shacklett, owned and operated Shacklett's Photography in Downtown Murfreesboro for more than four decades. This family business has for years recorded the lives and events of our community's citizens sharing their joys, sorrows, celebrations and calamities.

"Shack,"" Dick," "Richard" or "Claude" . . . you could tell how long someone had known him by the name they called him. Part of his daily routine was to settle around the City Café table with fellow businessmen and swap stories of what was happening in the 'Boro. He loved a good story... ANY story, but he REALLY loved to tell stories on himself. This is one that even after his death in 1994, some of those friends that gathered around the City Café table with him recounted to his son, City Councilman Bill Shacklett. (Bill and sister, Gloria Shacklett Christy continue to run the family photography studio.) Bill tells it like this:

Dad had just purchased a new, yellow Datsun station wagon and had gone by the gas station to fill it up. After getting the gas, he decided to run his new vehicle through the car wash to spiff up his new prized possession. As he drove around to enter the car wash, there appeared a couple of young college-aged guys that wanted to have their car washed, too. It appeared to dad that they were going to slip in front of him. That was NOT acceptable to this WWII veteran, he wasn't going to let these "whipper-snappers" get in front of him . . . SO he put the pedal to the metal and sped into the car wash ahead of the two young rivals. Content that he had won the race and the "old timer" still had something left in the tank, he relaxed to have the machine do its work.

The next thing dad saw was the rush of the water coming in his open windows filling the interior of his car. There was nothing for him to do but sit and take the punishment that followed. Pride cometh before the fall. Dad said that he looked in his rear view mirror to see the two guys laughing their heads off.

Life Lesson: Be sure you are right and then go ahead…. but make sure your windows are rolled up

+++

J. T. Burnett

Even though J. T. Burnett lived in Smyrna, he would drive to Murfreesboro several mornings a week just to join us at the community table. I, for one, was mighty proud he did.

J.T. worked for Woodfin's Funeral Home in Smyrna until his retirement. He loved poems and would cut them out of newspapers and other ephemera, or photo-copy them from books. And . . . here is the important part . . . he would send them to people. I was honored on more than one occasion to receive in the mail an envelope containing a poem J.T. thought I would enjoy. He was a thoughtful man.

After he became too feeble to drive himself to Murfreesboro, I visited him at his assisted-living home in Smyrna. He was always so happy to have a visitor, especially someone from the City Café gang.

J.T. was in the Navy during WWII and fought in the Pacific. He was on the island of New Guinea for quite a bit of time. This is one of the South Pacific Islands just above Australia that was known in earlier times for having head-hunter tribes.

This experience undoubtedly colored the story J.T. told about a missionary to New Guinea who was searching for a certain tribe. J.T.'s best-remembered story was a riddle that goes like this:

A missionary to New Guinea was trudging through the jungle in search of a certain village. The unique thing about this village is that all the men of it were known to always tell the truth. It was part of their religion. It was absolutely taboo to tell a lie. Consequently, the village was known as the Truth Tellers' Village.

Unfortunately, a nearby village was known as the Liar's Village for the same reason. All the men in that village always lied. They never told the truth.

The missionary had come as far along the trail as he could with the information he had to rely upon. He knew he was close but one more fork in the trail perplexed him. He didn't know which direction to take.

Fortunately, there was a native sitting right there in the fork of the trail. By his garb, the missionary knew he belonged to either the Truth Tellers' Village or the Liars' Village; they dressed the same, but he couldn't tell which the native was . . . a truth teller or a liar.

Now, here is the riddle: What single question did the missionary ask in order to determine which fork in the trail to take to get to the Truth Tellers' Village?

Now don't look further if you want to cogitate on this some.

Answer: He asked, "Which way is it to your village?" The truth teller has to tell the truth and point to the truth tellers' village. The liar has to lie and point to the truth tellers' village.

+++

An old menu

On the following two pages is a menu from City Café dated 1976. It's interesting to compare the evolution of the offerings and the prices! While its intriguing to fantasize about being able to get a meal at these prices today,

I did a comparison based on the federal government's inflation index and found that $1.00 in 1976 was the equivalent in buying power to $4.22 in 2016 (40 years later). Using the multiplier of 4.22, the cost of a meat & three vegetables ($1.95 for the most expensive) in 1976 is comparable to $8.23 today. Guess what? Today (2016) the City Café menu says a meat & three is $7.95 . . . a bargain!

A pie in '76 was 50¢. That would compute to $2.11 today. The actual price today . . . $2.25, not far off!

So, those of us who think the prices have gone up too high . . . apparently they haven't really changed at all.

City Café

Murfreesboro, Tennessee

Menu
Thursday Feb. 12, 1976

FRIED CHICKEN LIVERS with Cream Gravy...............1.75
ROAST PORK LOIN with Apple Sauce......................1.95
FRIED CHICKEN...1.65
COUNTRY STYLE STEAK, Brown Gravy...................1.85
ROAST BEEF, Brown Gravy....................................1.95

Choice of Three Vegetables

GREEN BEANS	TURNIPS
CONGEALED FRUIT SALAD	TOSSED SALAD
	BAKED APPLES
WHITE BEANS	PICKLED BEETS
COLE SLAW	MACARONI & CHEESE
MASHED POTATOES	CHOW CHOW PICKLE
POTATO SALAD	

••

HAMBURGER STEAK..2.00
RIBEYE STEAK...2.00
CLUB STEAK...2.25
T.BONE STEAK..3.00
    TOSSED SALAD, HOME MADE ROLLS,
    CHOICE OF BAKED POTATO OR FRENCH FRIES,

HOME MADE
CHILI...75¢
FRESH VEGETABLE SOUP..65¢
PORK BARBEQUE SPECIAL,
COLE SLAW, FRENCH FRIES, PICKLES.........................2.00
LUNCHEON SALAD BOWL..1.50
TOMATO STUFFED WITH CHICKEN SALAD OR
TUNA FISH SALAD..1.25

                CHERRY COBBLER............40¢
                LEMON ICEBOX PIE..........50¢
                HOME BAKED PIES...........50¢
                ICE CREAM......................30¢

+++

When the Simpsons owned the restaurant, Garry had a special menu he would sometimes jokingly put before a customer he knew had a good sense of humor and a strong stomach. (See following two pages)

+++

Café lá Roadkill

Eating food is more fun, when it was HIT ON THE RUN

Center Line Bovine..........................4.95
    "Tastes real good, straight from the hood"

The Chicken....................................3.95
    (That didn't cross the road)

Flat Cats...2.95
    Served in a stack, singles available

A TASTE OF THE WILD SIDE
(STILL IN THE HIDE)

Chunk of Skunk................................1.95
Smidgen of Pigeon............................1.95
Road Toad a lá Mode.........................1.65
Snake 'N Bake..................................2.25
Swirl of Squirrel................................1.55
Whippoorwill on a Grill.......................3.30
Narrow Sparrow................................1.25
Rigor Mortis Tortoise.........................6.75

CANINE SPECIALS
"You'll eat like a hog...when you taste our dog!"

Slab of Lab..2.95
Pit Bull Pot Pie.......................................1.95
Cocker Cutlets..3.95
Filet of Shar Pei....................................12.95
Poodles 'N Noodles.................................5.95
Snippet of Whippet..................................4.50
Collie Hit by a Trolley..............................3.95
German Shepherd Pie..............................3.95
Round of Hound......................................4.25

GUESS THAT MESS
A Daily Special Treat

If you can guess what it is...You Eat It For FREE!

LATE NIGHT DELIGHT
Rack of Raccoon.....................................3.95
Awesome Possum...................................1.95
Smear of Deer..4.95
Cheap Sheep..1.25
Served Fresh Each Night After Dark

+++

Politics

Some elected officials come into City Café regularly for a cup of coffee or a meal, and I applaud them because they are making themselves accessible to the public. Here, they get a pulse on the community; they find out, or confirm, what people are talking about that affects our community.

Some politicians only come in when there is a campaign going on. They shake hands, smile, kiss the babies, ask for your vote . . . and then you never see them again until the next election.

City Café has for years been a magnet for campaigners. Former owner, Garry Simpson, used to wear a big political button on his coat or shirt during these times that said, "I'm for YOUR candidate!"

He also sponsored a straw poll during each political campaign that has had quite a bit of notoriety. Quite a bit of accuracy, too! It has had a predictability rating of about 98%. (Of course, that's a statistic, and the reader will soon see where statistics rate among "True stories and other lies.")

One reason politicians showed up frequently during the straw poll event is because they got to vote every time they came in. One not-so-popular fellow running for city council came in a dozen time during the straw poll period. When the votes were finally counted, he had 12.

Owner Garry Simpson greets Gov. Lamar Alexander during a campaign stop at City Café. Garry's wife and co-owner, Pat, stands silhouetted at the window.

On the following page is a sample ballot used in one of the local election's straw polls. This particular one was modeled after the infamous "hanging chad" ballot made infamous in Florida's vote during the 2000 Presidential election.

OFFICIAL BALLOT

Rutherford County Primary Election
CITY CAFE
Murfreesboro, Tennessee

COUNTY EXECUTIVE
1. NANCY R. ALLEN (D) 1
2. GRANT KELLEY (D) 2
3. PAUL (STUMPY) NICHOLSON (D) 3
4. JIMMY EVANS (R) 4

TRUSTEE
5. EVANS MAPLES (D) 5
6. ANGELA H. BRANSBY (R) 6
7. JOHN P. EWALDSON (R) 7

SHERIFF
8. BARRY H. ASBERRY (D) 8
9. TRUMAN LEE JONES, JR (D) 9

CIRCUIT COURT CLERK
10. ELOISE GAITHER (D) 10

COUNTY COURT CLERK
11. WAYNE BAIN (D) 11
12. CHRIS BRATCHER (D) 12
13. BARBARA CUNNINGHAM (D) 13
14. GEORGIA ANN LYNCH (D) 14
15. DON WRIGHT (D) 15

REGISTER OF DEEDS
16. RAY GARRETT (D) 16
17. JENNIFER MEAGHER GERHART (D) 17

A busy day at City Café

Around Uncle Dave Macon Days, one might see a banjo picker in the Café. The blonde was singing along.

Typical group at the community table (circa 2014)
L to R: Don Sanders, Avent Lane, Ron Williams, Justin Lowe, Robert Holt, Matt Ward (author), Delmer Lowe

The New Generation
L to R: Jason N. King, attorney; Casey Rainey, stock broker; Chase Salas, insurance; Chris Gurley, insurance; Gabriel Frazier, insurance; Justin Howell, construction.

     The tradition continues with this group of young professionals. This group currently meets every Wednesday morning at City Café. However, they say they are not *gossiping*, they are *networking* with the goal of achieving *synergy* (the creation of a whole that is greater than the sum of its parts.) Yeah, right.

+++

City Café "10 O'clock" Coffee Club
Murfreesboro, Tennessee
December, 1993

The photo on the following page, now almost a quarter of a century old, still hangs on the wall of City Café with a plaque identifying the individuals as:

Back Row: Bill Carey, real estate; Henry Lane, candidate for sheriff; Boyd Dagley, insurance; Joe Christian, retired; Shirley Haley, ret. Firestone exec.; Bill Vogel, ret. broadcasting; Dale Hendrix, broadcasting; Terry Noah, ret. advertising; Ed Loughry, ret. banker; Cecil Henley, real estate;
Front Row: First man, unidentified; John McCreery, broadcasting; Earl Hull, stock broker; Robert Rose, ret. insurance exec.; Debby Bryson, waitress; Carl Thomas, ret. furniture rep.; Sammy Lester, farmer, real estate; Garry Simpson, owner City Café.

Matt Ward

Yeah, that's me, the compiler of this book. My nom de plume is Henry Matthew Ward. I've got four other books out under that name, so I used it on this one, too. But most people know me by Matt Ward.

I've told my share of accounts at the notorious table, too. And, naturally, I can remember more of them than I can recall of the other story tellers. So, here are some of them with apologies for monopolizing so much of this book.

A 25th Anniversary Dinner at City Café

Though most of the stories here are of a humorous nature, I can't write this book without telling of an event that truly touched my heart. When my wife and I were in college here back in the early '60s, we frequently came with friends to City Café for our evening meal. This was before we were married, just dating, but later, too. We married in 1963 just before my junior year at what was then MTSC.

Later, in 1988, after nine years away from Murfreesboro, and several more back here, I wanted to do something special for my bride of twenty-five years on our anniversary. I thought it would be romantic to take her out to dinner at the place we had first gotten to know each other, City Café.

The owners at this time were Garry and Pat Simpson. I arranged with them to have a table for two reserved with a red rose in a vase from Henry's Flower Shop sitting on it as an added touch. What made this evening so special, though, was what the Simpsons did without my knowledge.

At the appointed hour, I surprised my bride by stopping at City instead of continuing to some expensive restaurant as she, no doubt, expected. But, upon entering, I too was surprised to find that the Simpsons had put a white linen table cloth on the table and had set the table with fine china, silverware and crystal from their own home! Even a candle and linen napkins were there along with my little rose. I was touched to the point of tears! This was such an unexpected and kind thing for the owners to have done. We will never forget it.

The Simpsons had even alerted the local newspaper to what they thought the paper would find to be a human-interest story. They had a photographer come and snap our picture which, indeed, appeared in the Daily News Journal later that week.

Helen Dam's Wrong Turn

No, this isn't a story Helen told in City Café. It's one I told there on Helen.

Every Tuesday morning, Bob Parks Realty agents take off on its weekly tour of new listings. At the time, Helen Dam was one of our best agents and was the designated driver that week of one car full of agents.

Helen is the wife of Reverend Herman Dam. She liked to smile and tell everyone she was married to the Dam preacher.

At the time, Prudential Rowland & Wilson Realty also looked at its new listings on Tuesday morning. Danny O'Brien, a former Bob Parks agent who had become their broker was driving one car full of Prudential agents.

Helen was following BP agent Jim Walls' shiny white Oldsmobile 98. Danny O'Brien drives a shiny white Infiniti J-30.   The plot thickens........

Somewhere on the new stretch of Thompson Lane, Danny's caravan overtook the Parks' caravan. Passing Helen, Danny slid in behind Jim temporarily. Are you getting ahead of me, Reader?

Now, a big Olds 98 and a sporty Infiniti *do* look a lot alike....at least they're both white. So, when Danny turned at the next intersection onto Manson Pike, who can blame Helen for not noticing that Jim (and the rest of the Parks caravan) had continued across instead of turning. The rest of the Prudential group fell in behind Helen and thought it quite a coincidence that she seemed to be going their way.

It wasn't until they all pulled up in front of their new listing in Manson Retreat and Danny got out of his car with a quizzical look back at Helen parking right behind him, that she realized something wasn't kosher. "What's Danny O'Brien doing in the middle of our *Bob Parks* caravan?" she wondered. "Hmm, what's that Prudential sign doing in the yard of one of our listing?" "Who are all of these people getting out of their cars?"

"Uh-Oh, I think I made a boo-boo!"

"Danny! How fortunate! I just came by to preview this new listing of yours for a customer of mine. What a coincidence...driving up right when your caravan arrived!" (At least, that's the excuse she wished she had thought of, but didn't until a red-faced 5 minutes later as she raced to catch up with the other group somewhere out Franklin Rd.)

Actually, we all had a great laugh over it, and none more so than Helen. It's our fortune that it happened to such a good natured person with a great sense of humor that we can tell about it without fear of hurting her feelings.

The Insane Asylum

This story involves where I grew up, next to the insane asylum. (I hear some tacky witticisms being mumbled already as those who know me read the previous line.)

But, it's true. I did grow up next door to an insane asylum. It was called Central State Hospital for the Insane and was located on the southeast edge of Nashville on the corner of Murfreesboro Road and Donelson Pike. There was a corn field separating our little subdivision called Airport Estates, from the actual 19th century buildings that made up the hospital, but the field belonged to the hospital, so it literally was *the funny farm*.

The corn field sloped down into a dale in which there was an old spring house. It was about 12 feet wide and maybe 24 feet long. The stone walls were about 6 feet tall and it was filled with clear spring water, *cold* spring water. There was a tin roof over the structure that kept out all direct sunlight, but there were enough openings on the ends between the gabled roof and the stone wall to admit adequate light.

We neighborhood boys would sneak over the fence, cut through the corn field to the spring house and take a dip on hot summer days. Did I mention that water was COLD? It would take your breath away. One trip from one end to the other and back was all we could stand, thank you very much. But this is just a minor aside to the story I really want to tell about the asylum.

The earliest parts of Central State were built in 1852, and looked every bit as Victorian as the era. It had a guard house entry and an iron fence around the road frontage. In 1995 the hospital closed and moved to new facilities on Stewarts Ferry Pike. The original hospital was demolished in 1999 to make way for the new Dell Computer manufacturing plant. However, this story involves when I was a kid living nearby and the hospital was still the major insane asylum of Tennessee.

One day, a motorist on Murfreesboro Road was passing by the asylum when one of his tires had a blowout. He stopped right in front of the asylum and discovered he was going to have to change a flat tire. He followed the usual procedure, putting the lug nuts into the hub cap for safe keeping while he rolled the flat to the trunk and the spare to the vacant place. He had just positioned the spare onto the bolts of the axle plate when he stepped back and accidentally stepped on the hub cap holding the lug nuts.

All the lug nuts flipped over and fell into a highway drainage grate! Oh, no! The grate was far too heavy to lift and the openings in it were far too small to get his whole hand through to retrieve the essential nuts. He stood there a minute contemplating his situation and decided there was nothing to do but start walking.

Back in those days, the nearest service station was about two miles back toward town so that's the direction he headed. But, he didn't get more than a half dozen steps away from the car before one of the mental patients, who had been silently watching his dilemma through the fence, shouted out, "Hey, wait a minute!"

The motorist stopped and turned toward the patient who then calmly asked him if he was going to walk two miles to get help. "What other choice to I have?" the driver asked.

"Take one lug nut off of each of your other three tires and space them out on your spare. Then just take it easy until you can get somewhere you can buy some more." the patient explained.

"Well, of course!" the motorist shrugged. "Why didn't I think of that? . . . What are you doing in a place like this?" he added.

The patient replied, "They put me in here for being crazy . . . not for being stupid!"

Aunt Noval waits for my return

I've told this absolutely true story several times to different tables full (or is it tablesful?) of patrons at our eatery:

My wife had an aunt and uncle who never had any children. When the uncle passed away, we looked after the aunt as her substitute children. She moved to Murfreesboro and lived in a duplex practically right next door to us. She was legally blind by this time and had a Labrador guide dog.

One time she got a hankering to visit her brother who lived in Florida. Pat, my wife, couldn't go because she was tied up with concert work as a pianist at MTSU, so I volunteered to take her aunt. Aunt Noval wanted to take her guide dog along. (Remember this bit of information, it's important.)

We flew from the Nashville Airport. I dropped her, her guide dog, and our baggage off at the terminal and then circled the car back around into long term parking.

Once before, when Pat and I were flying somewhere, I wrote down the exact section and row I had parked in. I gave her the note for safe keeping. When we returned, however, she couldn't find the note anywhere, so I had to wander the parking lot looking for our car. It took at least a half hour of walking around before I found it.

This time, I wrote down the location again and kept it in a shirt notebook that I always carry around with me. When we returned from the four day visit, I reversed the procedure and left Aunt Noval on the curb pick-up along with her big Lab and our luggage. I rode the shuttle bus out to the parking lot and got off at the appropriate stop.

I looked at my note: "Parked in E2, 2nd aisle from Bus Stop 4 toward terminal." Clear enough! I walked over there, but couldn't find my car. I walked up and down that entire aisle looking at both sides of it for my car. I walked the next aisle and the next aisle. I re-read my note twice. I walked them again and then walked the aisles nearer the bus stop. Finally, I gave up. Someone had stolen my car, or else I had done something wrong in parking it and it had been towed. I stopped a shuttle bus and told the driver of my dilemma. She got on her two-way radio and called the terminal. They would send someone right out.

I waited five minutes...ten minutes. Aunt Noval had been waiting for probably 45 minutes by this time wondering what had happened to me. Finally, it dawned on me . . . didn't drive my car to the airport. I drove Aunt Noval's car because I didn't want to get dog hair all over my back seat. I rushed back over to where I first looked for my car and there it was — her car. I quickly got in and sped off before the airport assistance for dumb travelers arrived to laugh at my stupidity.

After re-reading the last paragraph, I realized other readers may be wondering, what's a legally blind person doing owning a car? It was a relic from her younger days when she could drive. She kept it so, if she had to impose on a friend to take her someplace, she could offer her car as the vehicle.

At least I didn't forget to go back up to the terminal to pick up Aunt Noval, the dog and baggage.

The Acupuncturist

Ron Williams (see his City Café tales elsewhere in this collection) swears by a Chinese lady acupuncturist in Nashville that he goes to for regular treatments. He's convinced it keeps a certain pain away that he would have otherwise suffered for years.

I've always wondered what it would be like to have an acupuncture treatment since it looks torturous, but everyone says it doesn't hurt in the least. Out of curiosity, I asked Ron for a referral to her and went when I had been experiencing some elbow pain for several weeks.

The lady had me take my shirt off and promptly declared "You rook rike Buddha!"

Hmph! My eyes don't look anything like his! Could she have been referring to my torso?

Well, she stuck pins in my back, my ankles, the tops of my feet, the back of my hands . . . everywhere but my elbow! I laid there for about a half hour with a heat lamp keeping those needles nice and warm while I listened to I guess what was the Chinese version of a Dixieland band on her stereo.

Finally, she came back in the room and removed the needles. I have to admit, they didn't hurt at all, but as to whether they were effective or not, I'm not impressed. The pain went away a day or so later all on its own and never returned.

Sit By Me

    Mark Wilson and I are the best of friends. Along with our wives, Susan and Pat, we have eaten out together at least once a week for over 25 years. We've vacationed together, laughed a lot and cried a little over the years.

    This friendship started in church at First Baptist. We all four sang in the chancel choir. Well, Pat actually was the pianist for it. And it was there that Mark pulled one of his best jokes on me.

    One Sunday, we lined up to go from the choir room to the choir loft in the sanctuary. As soon as we all sat down, I realized I had committed a faux pas. I had splashed on some aftershave lotion on my face that morning and I was supposed to abstain on Sundays because one of our sopranos was highly allergic to such fragrances.

    To make matters worse, Mark and I were the only two men on our row and we were sandwiched between the sopranos on my left and the altos on his right. I looked for the first time and realized I was practically right next to the lady with the allergy. I knew she must be suffering silently already.

    I whispered to Mark, "When we stand up for this first hymn, swap seats with me because I'm right next to Bertha and I forgot to leave off the aftershave this morning."

He nodded ascent. But then, unknown to me, he turned to the pretty college-aged girl on his right and said with a wink, "Matt wants to sit beside you."

As we rose for the first hymn, middle-aged man (me) slides next to the young co-ed whose eyes opened wide in half-shock, half-fear, half-repulsion (yes, that's three halves, but they were that wide)! I just smiled, not knowing what her problem was.

I did wonder why she swapped seats with a 70-year old lady on the second hymn.

Statistics

There are three kinds of lies: lies, damned lies, and statistics. The term was popularized in the United States by Mark Twain (among others), who attributed it to the British Prime Minister Benjamin Disraeli.

I suppose the reason statistics is considered the worst kind of lie is because they are true, yet more misleading than a lie. For example, like others, I have told the table the story of my first plane ride. It was in a 4-engine, prop plane that seated about 80 passengers. The year was 1960, and the occasion was to fly with the Nashville Post 5 American Legion band to the American Legion convention in Denver, Colorado.

    I was still in high school, but the band, made up of fine musicians who were service veterans needed a few extras to fill out instrumental parts that would otherwise have gone unplayed. My high school band director was in the Legion band and invited me and a couple of my bandmates to flesh-out the needed parts. We got to go, all expenses paid.

    The Post 5 American Legion band had some wonderful musicians in it. Several were present or former members of the Nashville Symphony. There was Sammy Swor, first trumpet with the symphony and director of Litton's Marching 100. Si Willis was a longtime percussionist with the symphony and prior to that was a pit drummer and xylophonist in vaudeville. Two Murfreesboro musicians, Dr. J. Madison (Pete) Dill, and his brother, Scobey Dill, who had played with some of the well-known big bands of the 40s like Tommy Dorsey and Glenn Miller, were playing cornet and clarinet respectively.

    These fine musicians comprised an excellent concert band and also occasionally played some marches for pass and review, but they virtually never marched themselves. Some of them were simply too old to march. We had one little fellow that played tuba and was a veteran of WWI. He must have been in his 80s. Si Willis was pushing 80, too.

Nevertheless, the band, in order to get a generous stipend from the National Headquarters of the American Legion to make the trip, had to participate in the parade and band competition. There were also drum and bugle corps that were sponsored by many of the Legion posts across the country. A couple of dozen of them were there to compete in their category.

The parade wasn't so bad. They must have had a lot of old veterans to consider who wanted to march, so the downtown Denver parade was only a few blocks long.

As a drummer, I wondered how we were going to supply a cadence, not having practiced any. Old Si wasn't perturbed a bit. He said he'd show me one when we lined up for it. Our drum line consisted of two snares (Si and me), a bass drummer and a cymbal player.

Standing in line, minutes before the step off, Si says, "You know the old German military beat?" Me: "Never heard of it." Si: "Well, it goes like this . . ." and he softly played a simple 16-beat ditty that did sound familiar and very easy to pick up. That, plus a standard roll-off to bring in the band, was all we needed. It was enough to keep the band in step and striking up on cue.

The laughable part was when it came to the band competition. We had to perform in two areas: one was a concert band piece. We were well prepared for that. The other, however, was performing on the field.

There were several required maneuvers for the field competition. A forward march, of course, a column right, column left, and counter-march (where the first rank of the band turns and marches down between the files of the remaining band members, then followed by the second rank doing the same thing 4 steps later, followed by the third rank, and so on until the entire block-band is marching back in the opposite direction from that in which they were going prior to the drum major's signal.)

We did about 5 minutes practice on these maneuvers prior to our time on the field, then managed to stumble through the routine for the judges.

The marching may not have been too impressive, but we played well a difficult repertory in the concert portion. When the competition was all over, we had managed to come in third. *Third in the Nation*, of all American Legion Bands!

And now, dear reader, the reason statistics rank behind lies and damned lies . . . there were only three bands in the competition!

My Favorite Room

I have told this one at City, but not too often because it's hard to get to the end without choking up.

In 1974, my wife, Pat, and I bought the house in which we still live. It was built in 1903 and by 1950 had been converted to 5 apartments. It had not been updated since that 1950 conversion. By this, I mean that the wallpaper had been there at least 24 years, probably longer, some was bubbling off the wall, all was dingy and faded; the ceilings had not only cracks, but areas where the plaster was completely missing right down to the lath board; floors were painted over and had knotholes where one could see the ground below. There were five kitchens and five bathrooms, but not a single shower, just tubs, some of them the old claw foot type. The kitchen we used while renovating had a sink so old that the hot and cold water came out of separate faucets.

We did most of the restoration ourselves. We could not have afforded craftsmen. Pat helped me with everything. Nothing was too dirty or unladylike for her to tackle. It took us until 1988, fourteen years, to complete the downstairs to basically what one would see today.

Being an old house with several antiques (now including us) passed down from family, I have been asked many times, "what was my favorite room?"

They all have their individual character and interest. I enjoy each of them virtually equally. "Whatever room I'm in!" was my standard reply, which I thought was rather clever, until I had an epiphany of sorts that made me realize what I enjoy most about each room and to where I gravitate.

I love to play a board game on the kitchen table with Pat. I love to sit in the library as we read a book or watch TV. I love to sit at my computer and write or read while she works at hers in the room we call our office. I love to sit in the music room and listen to her play the piano for literally hours on end. She doesn't practice so much as she simply plays for the sheer enjoyment of it.

Once again, while Pat was teaching a piano student in the music room, I was asked by the student's parent sitting in the sunny waiting room, what was my favorite room of the house. Just then, the mellifluous notes of a Chopin Etude Pat was demonstrating on the piano came drifting into our hearing. I had just gotten the words out, "Whatever room I'm in," when I stopped and thought. As my eyes misted over, I said, "No . . . it's not whatever room *I'm* in . . . it's whatever room *she's* in."

A Scary Florida Golf Course

Elsewhere in this collection of City Café stories you will find some golf tales. Golf stories are second only to fishing stories in that they should be heard with a skeptical ear. I promise, however, this next one is absolutely true.

I was playing a course in Florida. The first thing I experienced was some exotic, long-legged bird that was standing in the fairway about a 100 yards ahead of me and my Florida-resident playing partner.

"Don't hit that bird with your next shot." he said, "There's a $5000 fine for killing one of those."

Having previously busted the windshield out of a golf cart by blading a ball that I meant to gently loft over the cart parked between me and the green, I proceeded with apprehension. Well, outright nervousness, actually.

This Florida course was one of those that has residences surrounding it with their back yards abutting the course. I intentionally aimed well off to the side of where the bird was standing. It was too much. It went into one of those back yards.

As I went in to retrieve it, I saw what appeared to be an old, arching-type tombstone in the owner's back yard. "How weird," I thought, "almost macabre, to have a tombstone in the yard of this obviously up-scale home."

When I got close enough to read the inscription, it said:

Here Lie the Bones of the Last Golfer to Take a Divot Out of MY BACK YARD!

Yes, I picked up and took a drop!

An Albatross at the VA Golf Course

Another true golf story took place on the VA hospital's 9-hole course about 15 years ago. Don't let the title of this one confuse you into thinking I was referring to the sea gulls that have taken up residency at the nearby landfill (Mt. Trashmore).

I was playing with Dr. David Otts, who has a PhD in English and teaches math at MTSU (but that's another story). The two of us were putting out on the par-four 9th hole when a shot-gun like sound came from the direction of the 9th tee box. This was immediately followed by a golf ball rolling up to the edge of our green.

    I knew what had happened. There was a rise in the fairway between the teeing area and the green that was just high enough to hide the green from the view of the player in the tee box. If a tall player were to stand on a bench near the tee box, he could just barely tell if there were still players on the green and thereby wait longer to tee off (if he were a really long hitter).

    The single player that had been following us had evidently caught up to the extent he should have waited, but given the gap that we had maintained between us for the prior 8 holes, we should have had had enough time to have finished and walked off the course. He just assumed the coast was clear, but we had played that 9th hole so miserably that we were still there putting when his ball came sailing over the rise.

    Sometimes golfers get mad when a trailing golfer hits into them, but I couldn't resist having some fun with the situation. The VA course had no riding carts. Everyone walked. So, before he could walk far enough up the rise to see us on the other side, I ran and got his ball, took it over and . . . dropped it in the cup.

David and I scurried off the course and went into the clubhouse. We watched through a window as he approached the green looking all around for his ball. He even looked beyond the green before he finally walked over and looked down in the cup.

I can imagine what went through his mind. Elation at the discovery of a hole-in-one on a par four . . . a double eagle (aka albatross) . . . was tempered with the realization that he had no witnesses. He picked up his ball and came into the club house.

He asked us how long we had been there. "Oh, quite some time," I deadpanned.

"Did you see my last shot?"

"Nope."

The disappointment on his face was obvious, but probably not as bad as it would have been had we told him the truth. I almost hate to put this story into print. For the past 15 or so years, that fellow must have told dozens of his friends about his albatross on the 9th that fateful day. Now, he's liable to read this and it's going to shatter the memory of that moment of ecstasy.

The Helpful Waitress

One time, a little old lady came into City Café and ordered for her breakfast: coffee, bacon, grits and toast. The waitress, trying to be helpful and save her customer a little money, suggested she order the special which included all that plus two eggs and was priced cheaper than the al la carte order she had placed.

"But I don't want any eggs," the lady replied.

"But, it's cheaper!" the waitress reminded her.

"But, I don't want any eggs!" the lady protested.

"You don't have to eat them, just order the special and leave the eggs on the plate. You'll save 50¢!" the waitress whispered.

"Oh, very well. Give me the special," the customer acquiesced.

"How do you want your eggs?" the waitress asked.

"Raw and in the shell. I'll take them home!"

Old Age Ain't for Sissies

I went to a sleep clinic because of some issues with sleeping. They determined that I would be greatly benefited with a Continuous Positive Airway

Pressure machine, CPAP (pronounced cee-pap) for short.

    They gave me a prescription for one of the machines and gave me directions on where I could pick one up. I followed the directions and turned into a strip-mall area that had a stand-alone building near the rear of the strip. As I neared it, I could make out the name and the words *Oxygen and Crap*.

    "Crap?" I thought, "How unprofessional to use such language on the exterior of their building." When I got closer, I re-focused and realized it said OXYGEN AND CPAP.

    I'm going to get my eyes checked next week!

+++

Dwight & Barbara Faircloth

    One couple that frequented the café so often when Garry and Pat Simpson were owners was Dwight and Barbara Faircloth. Dwight had been a customer for years before his wife Barbara, who worked in LaVergne, finally took early retirement and was able to see what her hubby was talking about when he came home with stories and jokes heard at the tables there. They became such close friends with the Simpsons that they would mind the store for them on the rare occasion the Simpsons took a little time off.

Dwight is a big guy that used to be an airline agent. Everyone knows that he loves ice cream. But he says he only eats two kinds . . . homemade and store bought.

He also is a lover of southern gospel quartet singing and has booked groups of that genre for many venues. It was his wife, Barbara, though, who collected some of the stories and wrote them down for the Simpsons upon their retirement from City Café. Some are the same stories I have heard from the same sources. But, some I had never heard and yet they were too good not to include in this anthology. So, with Barbara's permission, I have quoted several of those from her booklet. They are identified with an asterisk (*) at the beginning of each.

*Dr. Eugene Cotey, former pastor of First Baptist Church, visited a man and invited him to church. The man told him he couldn't come because he didn't have clothes good enough to attend. So, Dr. Cotey raised some funds and took the gentleman to the Men's Shop and purchased a nice suit for him. The next Sunday he expected him to be at church but he wasn't.

So, he visited him and asked him why he didn't attend his church Sunday. The man replied, "I looked so good, I went to the Episcopal Church!"

+++

One-liners

Below is a collection of brief bursts of humor that may not rise to the level of *story*, but are deemed amusing enough to be included in this anthology of City Café utterances. Most of them are contributed by Barbara Faircloth (marked with the *).

Sammy Lester & Garry Simpson were sitting at the funeral of a third Café regular, Bill Vogle, as the preacher eulogized the deceased with multiple praises and commendations. Sammy punched Garry and said, "In a little bit, we need to go up there and see who's in that coffin!"

*Someone walked into the City Café about 8 AM and asked, "Where's Garry?" A regular customer replied, "He's gone out to get a decent breakfast."

*Jim Avaritt said he heard Norris Lovvorn singing in the City Café restroom and it was so bad the toilet flushed itself.

*Bill Nelms said a country preacher got a call to accept a position at a better-paying city church. He told his wife to start packing the dishes while he went upstairs to pray about his decision whether to accept or not.

*Pat Simpson said if she died, Garry would put her in the freezer until Sunday for her funeral because he wouldn't close the Café.

*Garry Simpson gave his wife, Pat, a meal ticket for her birthday.

*Pat says she only works half days – 12 hours.

*If a person get a bowl of vegetable soup and it has a lot of meat in it, Garry says he's going to have to charge for a "meat and three."

*Dan Bostaph was interrupted by Allen Richardson. Bostaph said, "Please let me finish." Allen responded, "I didn't know you ever finished – you never shut up!"

*Randall Chaudoin said Garry Simpson used to be *Gary* with one "r," but after he came to Murfreesboro, he got so uppity he changed it to 2 "r's"

*A VA outpatient asked Garry if he could use the telephone. He ordered a pizza and had it delivered to the City Café . . . and sat down and ate it there!

*A lady that, shall we say, was "less than fair-looking," came in and passed Garry heading for a booth. He whispered to Dwight Faircloth, "The crops must be harvested, the scarecrow is here." Dwight replied, "She is so ugly, the crows would bring back crops they stole 2 years ago!"

*Jim Avaritt said Larry Sims must have gone into counterfeiting. His ad says, "We will make you money if you let us."

*Garry greeted Hot Air (Bobby Winn) with, "What do you know?" Hot Air said, "Nothing." Garry replied, "I was just confirming it."

*C. Ray Carter passed around a photo of himself and his dog asleep on the couch. When shown the picture, four different people asked, "Which one is the dog?"

*Jim Avaritt made the comment one morning that he had sat at the table so long that his coffee was almost warmed up enough to drink.

*When Pat Simpson wants to know some gossip or something that is really none of her business she says, "Are you going to tell me the truth, or do you want me to tell it my way?"

Fran Pierat, a long-time waitress at City Café, sometimes came across like a drill sergeant in the mess hall. People were so used to the banter with waitresses and management that she could get away with things that would have been insults worthy of firing elsewhere. Once, she put the wrong plate of food down in front of a customer. When he said this wasn't what he ordered, she barked, "You'll eat it, and *like* it!"

*Dale Hendrix nagged Barbara Faircloth and Pat Simpson for a month to make him a coconut cake for his birthday. Well, on his birthday, Barbara arrived with a white cake box and Dale was overjoyed. He said, "Look! Here comes my cake!" All that was inside was an apron and a coconut, along with a big note that read, "Hey, Dale, make your own damn cake!"

Someone asked one of the Presbyterians if he believed in free will. "Of course, I do!" the Calvinist replied. "I have no choice!"

Garry was once asked how many employees worked at City Café. He answered, "About half of them."

As I drove into the block of East Main the City Café is on, I realized it was a busy day downtown. It looked like every parking space was taken. I said to myself, "Lord, if it's meant for me to have my coffee and fellowship at the Café today, there will be a parking space left for me." And sure enough, on the 10th time around the block, there it was!

+++

A Brief History of City Café

Many small towns and cities have an eatery called City Café. The name is almost generic for the typically family run "meat & three" genre of restaurants. A quick check on the internet discovered one in all these Tennessee cities: Chattanooga, Cleveland, McMinnville, Brentwood, Nashville, Morristown, Munford, Smithville, Dickson, Cumberland City, Lexington, Newbern, Hohenwald, Celina and Dayton. And this wasn't even an exhaustive search. There are multiple City Cafés in virtually every state.

The restaurant that was to evolve into City Café was opened by brothers Dorsey & Henry Cantrell in 1900 and was located on the south side of the public square. At that time, it was known as Cantrell's Restaurant. The Cantrells also owned a dairy in the Salem Community of Rutherford County. In the 1920s, Cantrells' dairy hauled raw milk to the square where they processed and bottled it upstairs above the restaurant.

The following page shows a picture of the south side of the public square circa 1900. The small white sign in the lower right corner says, "David & Cantrell Lunch Room."

About ten years later, in the early 30s, brother Henry Cantrell moved the milk bottling process to a new location on College St. That left the upstairs at Cantrell's Restaurant on the public square's south side available for other pursuits, and did they ever pursue them! Prohibition had just ended in 1933. The upstairs became a drinking and gambling venue!

About this time (early to mid 30s), Cantrell's Restaurant changed the name to City Café. They punned the restaurant's new name by spelling it *City Calf A* in some advertising media. Perhaps, this was to pay homage to Rutherford County's leading industry at the time (dairies) and of course the Cantrells' own dairy.

Quoting from a Daily New Journal article of November 8, 2014:

In July 1936, George Snow, Albert Dubois and several others were gaming above the café. Patsy Henson remembers that her uncle (Snow) was a skilled gambler and that he was said to be winning big on the evening of July 12, 1936.

"Uncle George left the game for a break and Dubois followed him out," recounts Henson. According to newspaper accounts, a "cutting fray" resulted and Snow was mortally wounded. Dubos was eventually

convicted of manslaughter and served 14 months of a 10-year sentence.

1936 was also the year the City Café hired its first waitresses, sisters Audie and Sara Overall and Peggy Brown. Prior to that, the Cantrell family did all the service.

C.B. Arnette, in his book *From Mink Slide to Main Street*, told of working as a waiter there for a brief period in 1936. He said that the wage scale for a new waiter was $7.00 and all the food he could eat. Oh, that was not $7 per hour, not even $7 per day. That was for a 69-hour week and before the luxury of air-conditioning. But, that was deep in the depression era. The food alone was probably worth the work.

The menu at that time included hamburgers, 10¢; ham and wiener sandwiches, 10¢; ham and egg, 15¢; triple-decker club sandwich, 25¢.

Arnette recalls that his friend, Hollis Westbrooks (later to become mayor of Murfreesboro) remembered Grand Ole Opry legend Uncle Dave Macon came into the City Café one day. The owner, Uncle Dorsey (as Cantrell was known) introduced him to the other customers and asked him to "tell us a big lie." Uncle Dave promptly stated that, "this was a good place to eat!"

In 1946, Cantrell sold his business to two brothers, Sewell and Price Manley.
This ownership lasted only 5 months, selling it to C. L. Hall.

Initially, Hall kept it for only about a year himself before trading it to Lester Mason, for Mason's farm in the Mona community (Jefferson Pike area) who took ownership in April of 1948.

Mason claimed restaurant experience "up north," but his restaurant business here did not prosper and by 1950 Hall had resumed ownership. Whether Hall had financed a portion of the business (the farm not sufficing for an even trade) is not known. Perhaps he foreclosed, or they swapped back because neither was satisfied with their career change. At any rate, C. L. Hall became the owner again . . . or, it was never really out of his ownership as a contract for deed would provide. In a contract for deed, the buyer doesn't get clear title deed until certain conditions have been met.

This time Hall partnered with another former owner, Sewell Manley. Within a year, however, they closed the café which had been open for just over 50 years at this 11 South Side of Square address.

For those readers who are trying to place where 11 South Side of Square is, the businesses that followed City Café (nee Cantrell's Restaurant) in that location were (beginning in 1950): Stroud's Appliances, then Singer Sewing Machine Company which operated there until 1984. It was followed by Marti and Liz Shoes and is currently occupied as an annex to Binks Outfitters (the building adjacent to the drive-through for Big B Cleaners).

Now comes the fly in the ointment. There was a two-year gap between City Café closing on the square and City Café opening on East Main St. under a different owner.

The closing of then owner C.L. Hall's City Café, left the square with only two restaurants, the L&M Café at 125 S. Church and Vincent DeGeorge's Italian fare restaurant. The bulk of the remaining eateries were located in the first block of East Main. There was Kenneth's Snack Shop (Bessie Shipp, owner) at 113 E. Main, DeGeorge's Soda Shop at 121 E. Main, Cook's Café just around the corner at 108 N. Spring St.

Then there was one more, Andrew Tamburo, an Italian immigrant had already opened Andrew's Café at 121 East Main in 1924, but had moved it to 107 East Main in 1936. With that new location, he changed the name of his restaurant from Andrew's to Dixie Café.

In 1954, two years after the restaurant at 11 South Side of Square had closed, Tamburo changed the name of his restaurant. He took the no longer used or claimed name, City Café.

This 107 E. Main location is where the new City Café remained beyond Tamburo's death in 1956 when the restaurant was acquired by Maurice and Pauline McKnight. That was also the year Shipp's restaurant moved across the street and became Shipp's Wagon Wheel Café. Shipp's former location at 113 E. Main became Pat & Mike's Café.

Ernest and Ethel Watson took over the City Café in 1958. Their tenure lasted 23 years until 1981 when Frank and Helen Cooper bought the business.

The Coopers ran it for 5 years and sold it to Garry and Pat Simpson.

Many people that habituate our Murfreesboro City Café, don't realize it isn't still where it was when they ate there years ago. The restaurant was located at 107 East Main St. for about 40 years, but in 1992, then owners, Garry and Pat Simpson purchased 113 and 115 East Main and moved the business there. They did extensive renovation creating openings between the two adjacent buildings and utilized the upstairs of the 113 building for meetings such as the Gideons who meet up there regularly. In all, the Simpsons virtually doubled the seating capacity by moving to the new location.

The Simpsons did much to preserve the traditions of City Café . . . the casual dining, the home-style fare, the community table, the rolls, the old cherry hutch (moving it to the new location), and the friendly relationship they maintained with their customers. They were on a first-name basis with all of their regulars. Dozens of customers considered the Simpsons their personal friends. Many were so trusted that, if the Simpsons were busy, they rang up their own meals on the cash register.

In a newspaper interview, Pat Simpson was quoted as saying, "Really, we don't own the City Café. It belongs to the people here. Garry and I just have the privilege of being the caretakers."

Mr. Nelson Smotherman compiled this handy lineage of ownership of the City Café plus the dates and locations of the café:

Dorsey J. & Henry Cantrell
11 South Side of Square
2/10/1900 to 12/1/1946

Sewell & Price Manley
11 South Side of Square
12/1/1946 to 5/1/1947

Claude & Lela Hall
11 South Side of Square &
107 East Main St.
5/1/1947 to 1952

Maurice & Pauline McKnight
107 East Main St.
1952 to 1957

Ernest & Ethel Watson
107 East Main St.
1957 to 1985

Frank & Deane Cooper
107 East Main St.
1981 to 1985

Garry & Pat Simpson
107 & 113 East Main St.
1985 to 2007

Scott & Scarlett Perkins
113 East Main St.
2007 to 2014

Tammy Greer & Teresa Kellogg
113 East Main St.
10/1/2014

+++

Stifanina Tamburo Hayden

The Tamburos, the reader will recall, were the owners of the Café when they established it at 107 E. Main in 1936 initially under the name of Dixie Café. Their daughter, Stifanina Tamburo Hayden, told of growing up in the restaurant. She remembered as a toddler sleeping in the candy case beneath the cash register. She said they had big stalks of bananas hanging that sold for 5¢ a dozen.

She recalled that her parents always used fresh produce and usually ground their own meat. Her dad was noted for his chili and barbequed ham. There was a solid marble fountain counter from which they served hand-dipped ice cream and milk shakes. Behind it was a cherry and marble hutch with leaded glass windows that is still used today. [The huge (now antique) hutch was moved to its present location at 113 E. main when the café relocated again, and sits behind the cashier.]

Stifanina remembered that when the Rutherford County area was used as a "maneuver training area" for the army in 1941, the café was packed nightly with soldiers pining for a home-cooked meal.

"A normal breakfast order consisted of 2 eggs, 4 pieces of bacon, and 2 pieces of toast. One soldier came in and ate six full orders!"

Ernest and Ethel Watson

The Watsons took over the Café in 1957. They had been in the restaurant business since the early '40s. Earnest had worked in the old Sally Ann Bakery and put his experience to work creating the famous City Café rolls. [But, see the following story on Brown Sanford who perfected them.]

When they started, the country ham plate lunch was the most expensive meat & three offering. It cost 85¢. A hot roast beef sandwich with mashed potatoes was 40¢.

The Watsons were the first proprietors to introduce the meal ticket plan which gave a 20% savings on meals. They never advertised, but frequently had lines out the door waiting for lunch tables.

Near the end of the Watson's tenure with the Café, Middle Tennessee State University students had developed such an affinity for the place they dedicated part of their 1979 yearbook, The Midlander, to it. [The reader may recall, this author mentioned that he and his future bride ate many a meal at the City Café in the early 1960s with other student friends. This would have been during the Watsons' era.]

1981 Retirement party for Watsons

Brown Sanford
The Roll Man

    This is not so much a story heard in City Café as it is a story about City Café and one of the cooks that made it so popular.

    Brown Sanford became the cook at City right after he got out of the Navy in 1955. His wife had been cook prior to that, but the family was growing (eventually to 8 children), so she stayed home and he took over the restaurant's kitchen.

    His magnum opus was his rolls! He experimented with many recipes until he had it just right. Many patrons have said it was the aroma of his mixture of yeast, water, salt, sugar, shortening and eggs baking in the oven that brought them into the restaurant the first time, and brought them back! The rolls were so popular that customers have been known to walk out without ordering if the day's batch had been depleted.

    In his hey-day, Brown would get to the restaurant at 3 AM and start mixing the ingredients. By dawn, he had copious blobs of dough rising that he would catch just before they spilled over the stainless steel bowls. He would punch each down a half dozen times during the morning before finally pinching off fistfuls and dropping them into muffin pans to begin the baking.

I can't say enough about the fragrance of those freshly baked rolls. As it wafted outside, it was as enticing as the Sirens of Greek mythology who lured sailors to their death on the rocks of the seashore. In this case, it was death by yeast roll ecstasy!

He used 100 pounds of flour every day in making about 100 to 110 dozen rolls for the lunch and supper crowds. The recipe has remained a secret. Owner Garry Simpson used to say he had it locked up in a safe (and point to his head).

+++

Nadine Cantrell

Nadine Cantrell worked at City Café for nearly a half century. She started in 1940 when the café was still on the south side of the square.

It was there she met her husband to be, James "Doc" Cantrell. He was a waiter working for his family, the owners of City Café at the time. They married three days after the infamous date of Dec. 7, 1941.

By the late 1980s, she was the petite old waitress who would wait until closing time and then crawl under a table to retrieve a nickel she had spotted during the day. She and her husband never owned a car, never had any children, never took vacations, lived in a very modest house and had few amenities.

One day, some young hoodlums broke into her house and stole about $25,000 that she had squirreled away in a Ball jar kept in a chifferobe in her bedroom.

The newspaper reported that she had been robbed of her life-savings. Donations came in from customers and strangers alike. People came by City Café and wanted to leave money for her, not just tip money, but $10, $20, $100.

At first, Garry Simpson, the café owner at the time, tried to tell the benefactors that she was in good shape. She would weather the storm just fine. Well, you would have thought he was Ebenezer Scrooge telling them that Tiny Tim lacked for nothing. Finally, he acquiesced and starting accepting donations for Nadine.

But, you see, Garry knew something the customers didn't know, the newspaper didn't know, and the donors didn't know. Nadine was a bona fide millionaire!

Her husband was just as frugal as she was and put every penny of his check as an employee at the VA

Hospital into a savings account. They lived on her income alone and didn't even use all of it. They saved and invested. Garry had helped them some with their investments and that's how he knew how much Nadine was really worth.

Granted, $25,000 is a lot of money to most of us, but it represents only 2.5% of a million. There are plenty of stock market investors that lose 2.5% of their net worth in a day of bad trading on Wall Street. Who donates to them to make up the loss?

Now, don't go stiffing your waitress just because of this story. Most of them aren't millionaires, just hard working people, on their feet all day, taking abuse for the cook's mistakes as well as their own human errors, who are making less than $3 per hour unless they get your tip.

+++

Garry & Pat Simpson

The Simpsons owned the café for 22 years. Garry had been a regional supervisor for Waffle Houses for several years prior to deciding to invest his time and knowledge in a place of his own. He and Pat were a perfect match for the demands of the City

Café. They respected its traditions, were friendly and outgoing, worked and played well together. Garry would arrive at 6 AM, Pat handled the lunch crowd, Garry would be back at 2:30 PM until closing at 7 PM (plus time to put things back in order). In addition to Pat's time at the Café, she took kids and eventually grandkids to school, baby sat and maintained the household.

Lots of celebrities have eaten at City Café. Just off the top of his head Garry could remember Lamar Alexander, The Charlie Daniels Band, Porter Wagner, Jerry Reed, Ronnie Stoneman, Rose Ann Cash, Marty Stewart, Archie Campbell, Sharon Puckett, and of course Hank Williams, Jr. who did a video-taping promo there for a Monday Night Football.

Both had the personality to cajole customers in a way the customers enjoyed the teasing and would want to come back for more.

Throughout their 22 years, prices had to go up with inflation, but quality and quantity never went down. The greatest risk at City Café was overeating!

Toward the end of their tenure, Pat started having health issues and this prompted their decision to sell and retire. Granddaughter, Deja, who worked there as a waitress for them, predicted that "Grandpa will become one of those *City Café story tellers,* sitting at the community table trying to top the rest of them!"

But, retirement didn't agree with the metabolism of the Simpsons. A couple of years after selling City Café, they started looking around for another similar operation in Middle Tennessee. They wanted something they could share the work and knowledge they had gained with their son, Chris. They found it on the square in Shelbyville. A place called Pope's had been closed for a while and was for sale.

They re-opened it, kept the name, and tradition. Now, it's getting the same rave reviews that they garnered in Murfreesboro. Son, Chris and his wife run the café. Garry and Pat still keep a hand in it because it seems they are bored without that outlet for their energy. At the same time, they have passed a heritage on to the next generation.

+++

Tammy Greer

As this book is being written, the current owner of *City Café* is Tammy Greer. Her parents, Bill and Pat Crowder, owned and operated the Midway Diner at Deason.

For those of you familiar with the Midway Diner, there's an interesting story how it got its name. It is not because of the location between Murfreesboro and Shelbyville of which it is much closer to Shelbyville.

When Tammy was just a child, her parents lived in Smyrna but attended church on the far side of Shelbyville. Each trip to and from church, as they passed Deason her dad would say, "Well, we're midway there." Later, when he got a chance to invest in a restaurant in Deason, he named it what he had called the spot for years . . . Midway. Was it fate, or faith that named that diner?

Tammy worked in all capacities in her parents' restaurant, which was very similar in style and fare to City Café, so she came with a solid background in the business.

She and her good friend, Teresa Kellogg, initially bought the restaurant from the Perkins and were co-owners. But, nearly a year into their ownership, Teresa learned she was about to be made a grandmother the second and third time over. She decided she wanted to retire from the restaurant business and go full-time into grandmothering.

Tammy amicably bought out Teresa and became the sole proprietor of City Café.

+++

There are, no doubt, many other stories that are as funny, or touching, or informative that have been told in this iconic eatery. If I sat a while longer, I'm sure more would come to mind, and I'm sure other patrons could add some lulus that I didn't get to hear because I left too early or got there too late. Keep telling 'em, friends; that's half the reason for the café's longevity. And have some good "home cooking" while you do. But, don't talk with your mouth full!

Bon Appétit